BACKWARDS Beliefs

"Danison presents an account of spiritual beliefs gleaned from her near-death experience. . . . In her third book concerning near-death experiences, the author sets out to compare the spiritual truths she learned during the experience with ideas from organized religion. . . . Readers interested in near-death experiences may find the book compelling for its depiction of reality, but those who don't accept Danison's experience at face value will struggle with the text."—**Kirkus Book Reviews**

"What a fascinating and disturbing book (in a good way)." **Editor, FATE Magazine**

BACKWARDS and BACKWARDS Guidebook

"*BACKWARDS* . . . is an examination of this phenomena [NDE] in which it's questioned thoroughly with an educational eye, with a focus on the case of a true story of a big time lawyer being on the brink . . . . *BACKWARDS* is deftly written and researched, and highly recommended."–**Midwest Book Review**

"Forward thinking is fine in all, but one can find many answers just by looking back. '*Backwards Guidebook*' is a second in a series called '*Backwards*.' Asking many of life's questions, ranging from God to the meaning of life, Danison and company keep it secular while waxing philosophical in ways that will tax the mind, but leave it better from the exercise. A strong choice for those looking for answers about life, the universe, and everything, '*Backwards Guidebook*' is a definite purchase for those who have read the first and enjoyed it."—**Midwest Book Review**

"Consistent with works such as Conversations with God and A Course in Miracles, *Backwards* clarifies and simplifies the complexities that we tend to manifest into our lives."—**TCM Reviews**

"[A]re we all going to have to wait until we pass across to discover what that experience really is? In Nanci L. Danison's book these questions subside: here is a writer who is trained in observing and listening and summarizing and convincing as only a fine trial lawyer can. . . . [T]he author is very much worth reading and heeding."— **Grady Harp, Amazon Top 10 Reviewer**

"'*Backwards: Returning to Our Source for Answers*' will be well received by students of metaphysics, self improvement, and readers in the genre of spirituality. However, because of the nature of the material, there will be controversy and opposition from traditional academics, physicians, scientists, and theologians."–**Reviewer's Bookwatch**

"This is a book that lets you know what a near death experience is like and it will amaze you. The book will startle you with revelations that you never thought of and this is easily one of the most controversial books I have ever read. I am not sure I agree with it but it certainly gives me a great deal to think about."—**Amos Lassen, Amazon Top 100 Reviewer**

"Nanci went farther than most NDErs. . . . She looked at life, and death, from multidimensional perspectives—the human, the soul, the Light Being, and Source. . . . If you read just one new book about NDEs this year, make it this one."—**Vital Signs Magazine**

"Danison's elaborate but very readable story is summarized in her first book, '*Backwards: Returning to Our Source for Answers*' (A.P. Lee, 2007), and discussed more formally in her new book, '*Backwards Guidebook*' (Lee, 248 pages, $15.95). She spent many months taking notes from memory, recording as much as she could recall from her experience. . . . It's a pretty tough observation, which to me lends credibility: Danison is just telling us what she learned—no sugar-coating."—**The Spokane Spokesman-Review**

BACKWARDS BELIEFS

Also by Nanci L. Danison

Books

BACKWARDS: Returning to Our Source for Answers
BACKWARDS Guidebook

Audiobook

BACKWARDS: Returning to Our Source for Answers

DVDs

Be Your Own Psychic
Interview by Ted Henry (ABC News)
Manifesting: Creation, Not Attraction
Meaning of Life
Nanci Danison at the Edgar Cayce A.R.E.
Our 5 Spiritual Superpowers
What Happens When We Die?

CDs

God Loves, Man Judges
How to Access Universal Knowledge
How to Manifest Physical Reality
Life Plan From the Afterlife
Manifest Consciously with Unconditional Love
Primer on Life and Death
Purpose of Life
Revelations
Self-Healing

BACKWARDS BELIEFS

Revealing Eternal Truths
Hidden in Religions

Nanci L. Danison

A.P. Lee & Co., Ltd., Publishers
Columbus, OH

AP Lee & Co., Ltd., Publishers
PO Box 340292
Columbus, OH 43234
"Evolving mankind, one book at a time."

Library of Congress Control Number:
2011929908

ISBN-13: 1-978-934482-10-0

Contents

Acknowledgments

S OME OF THE TALENTED PEOPLE who have helped me produce this third *BACKWARDS* book include: my editor Erin Clermont; my peer reviewers Andy Hoye, Chuck Swedrock, and Jack Rued; Chip Eggerton, the genius graphic designer who created the cover graphic; Jay Cookingham with Holy Fire Publishing, who designed the cover and dust jacket; Karen Lynch, author photographer extraordinaire; and my friends and family at A.P. Lee & Co., Ltd., who never fail to support me. A special thanks is extended to the authors and publishers who have allowed me to weave their thoughts and words into my text in support of my own personal experience.

I especially want to thank the readers who have written to me with questions. I hope each of you wonderful Light Beings knows how much your interest and support sustain me.

My Death

I DIED AT AGE FORTY-THREE of either anaphylactic shock from a local anesthetic injection or of severe hypoglycemia, or a combination of the two.

Briefly, I was in a nationally acclaimed cancer hospital to have three suspicious lesions removed from my right breast. Right before the surgery, a radiologist performed a needle localization procedure, using mammograms to locate the lesions and mark the area for the surgeon to remove. The procedure entailed inserting a large bore needle with a wire inside it into my breast under local anesthetic, and then withdrawing the needle to leave the wire in place. The position of the needle was adjusted several times to get the wire deep enough. Each adjustment required a new mammogram to check position. After seven or eight mammograms, the radiologist and technician left the room. Shortly thereafter, my blood pressure dropped to nothing and my heart stopped. I left my body and went into the afterlife.

The details of my afterlife experience are recounted in my first two books: *BACKWARDS: Returning to Our Source for Answers* and the *BACKWARDS Guidebook*. All the answers I received from Universal Knowledge about who God is, who I am, heaven and hell, the purpose of life and why we were created are explained there as well.

I

Dying to Know Where Religion Fits In

HAVE YOU EVER WONDERED WHETHER your religious or spiritual beliefs are true? I used to—until dying opened my eyes to a reality I could never have imagined.

The afterlife I lived bore little resemblance to the heaven glorified by the priests and nuns of my school days. True, life after death was indescribably blissful, loving and saturated with unconditional acceptance. But little else matched my expectations forged through religious education. My deceased father, sisters, and grandparents were not there to greet me. No angels shepherded me through "crossing over." I did not see Jesus, Mary, or any other religious figure. Heaven revealed no sumptuous gardens, golden cities, or physical environment at all. In short, I witnessed nothing that reflected my religious training—though I experienced a wealth of unanticipated otherworldly delights.

What was not delightful, however, was finding out that humans had constructed most of my religious beliefs—not God. Before I died, I believed the Word of God was revealed to various historical religious leaders and passed down through the ages. The reality I faced, indeed lived for quite some time before returning to human life, is that in many ways religious history is backwards—both primal and the opposite of what actually happened. Hidden beneath the patina of honest human misunderstanding, however, gleam tiny nuggets of eternal truth about our Creator, the universe, and our true purpose in life. All we have to do to find them is look with spiritual eyes. Our reward is spiritual and emotional treasure beyond our wildest dreams.

I was not a particularly mystical person before I died. But I did have extensive religious education. My background includes twelve years of traditional Roman Catholic elementary and high school. I studied religions of the world in a Methodist college while earning a Bachelor of Science degree with double majors in biology and chemistry, investigated converting to Judaism while earning a Bachelor of Arts degree in psychology, and attended Catholic mass on and off during my first sixteen years practicing law in a 270-attorney regional law firm. My long-standing beliefs encompassed all the Judeo-Christian tradition and history handed down through the ages. Yet none of this prepared me for the reality of the heaven I entered.

My heaven was an intellectual paradise rather than a physical one. There, in the Light, an incredible wealth of information—what I now call Universal Knowledge—downloaded, in effect, directly into my mind, filling me with answers to all my questions about the meaning of life. Answers that were in many ways the opposite of our commonly accepted religious beliefs. I learned the objective truth about God, what I now call Source, as well as who I am in relation to Source. I witnessed firsthand why and how the universe was created. I was shown that there is no heaven or hell as humans commonly conceive of them. And I came to understand our true purpose on Earth, as well as the manifested nature of human bodies and how we inhabit them as "Light Being" souls.

The Universal Knowledge instilled in me resonated as so much more believable, and more wonderful, fulfilling, reasonable, and soothing than my belief system of forty-three years, that my mind reeled with the contradictions between the answers I got in the hereafter and those I learned in school. My surprise upon discovering new truths about life and death sparked righteous anger deep within me. Before dying, I believed that in the afterlife we would no longer feel negative emotions. Yet, I did feel anger. I keenly resented that this comforting knowledge had not been readily available to me— and to everyone else. Even the bliss of intimate proximity to Source could not soothe the heartsickness I felt, like I had been betrayed by my religious education.

Desperately wanting to know why nothing I had encountered so far in the afterlife meshed with worldwide religious beliefs, I sought Universal Knowledge on why my religion taught me what I now recognize as obvious humanizations of eternal truths. The answer arrived as a panoramic vision of the history of planet Earth highlighting the role religion has played in mankind's development.

Unlike the other wisdom infusions, where all knowledge on a topic exploded into my mind as a global understanding, the story of religious history was presented chronologically, as if it were a documentary film. Telepathic explanations accompanied the visual experience. A visual timeline layered above the documentary showed Earth's lifespan clearly divided into three epochs. I actually heard the word "epoch" in my mind, though nearly everything else I learned in the afterlife was communicated without language.

The vision of history came fast and furiously, permeated with intricate, fascinating, and completely wondrous scenes of life on Earth. The details of thousands of developments in religious dogma, intertwined like links in a chain with the rise and fall of thousands of religions, were nestled within the life story of Earth as a human habitat. This afterlife perspective disclosed to me very different events than appear in the scriptural history I had read.

As I silently observed mankind's evolution, and witnessed

firsthand how religions had impacted that journey, my heart filled with understanding and unconditional love. Like newborn babes, generation after generation breathlessly reached out to the universe for answers and guidance. And, like toddlers, they wobbled and often fell. I saw the tapestry of superstition, mythology, and misunderstanding humans had woven into religious dogma to which they still cling with the tenacity of shipwreck survivors. Yet man's attempts to understand basic kernels of truth are so earnest, and their hearts so full of longing, I could not help but love each and every person. My earlier anger was forgotten. In essence, I had transcended human emotions and taken Source's attitude toward religious history—unconditional love of every faltering step mankind takes in its quest to understand life itself.

I learned that Source has not been silent for thousands of years. All of human history sparkled with messengers radiating love and truth, like the sparklers I twirled on July Fourth evenings of my youth. I had been taught in parochial schools that God's messages to us were delivered thousands of years ago. On the contrary, our Creator gives us new messages every day—some via courageous souls who survive literal death. Each soul that separates from its dying host and enters the afterlife, however briefly, and then returns to human life brings new words of truth and comfort. Viewing history from Source's perspective revealed millions of messengers over the ages. To my immense surprise, they were not church leaders, prophets, kings—or anyone whose name I had ever heard, except for Gene Roddenberry, the creator of the StarTrek TV series. Rather, these messengers appeared in the form of regular people: artists, filmmakers, singers, musicians, authors, schoolteachers, office workers, homemakers and open-minded, loving people of all descriptions.

For years after my death I puzzled over how my former religious beliefs could have so missed the mark. The contradictions between what I had gleaned from religious texts and what I beheld with my own eyes in the afterlife documentary haunted me. I wondered whether I was the only one in the world to have been given such a devastatingly different perspective on religious history. So I began to research. My years of research have uncovered two rich resources that have brought me peace.

My first step was to find out whether other afterlife experiencers had received the same history lesson I had. I knew that millions of people had personally experienced some degree of life after death and lived to tell about it. Some have written books or articles describing what medical experts call a near-death experience, or NDE for short. (Appendix.)

After reading many near-death and afterlife reports in books and on the Internet, I found many people remember with crystal clarity the Universal Knowledge they absorbed during their sojourns in the Light. The data they received runs the gamut from insights about their own and loved ones' futures to entire bodies of knowledge on diverse topics, like a new physics model or healing methodologies. A few experiencers recount, each in his or her unique way, the same truths about life and death that were revealed to me. All Universal Knowledge recipients report being convinced of the truth of the secrets shared in the Light. I know I am convinced because I personally lived what I learned.

Those experiencers who remember being immersed in Universal Knowledge often attribute it to direct communication with a Being of Light, or with God, Jesus, angels, or other religious figures. I was told that Universal Knowledge is presented in the form most easily accepted by the newly arrived soul. A few experiencers have described it as I do—as instantaneous "knowings"—information downloaded as a whole directly into their minds from a body of wisdom that encompasses the universe.

At various points in my afterlife journey knowings washed over me in waves of complete understanding. Everything that could possibly be known paraded through my mind in an instant. I understood that I at last knew everything there was to know. I was omniscient! For a moment. No language was used. Knowings were communicated as a collage of images, sounds, emotions, intuition, and experience, plus through another intangible level of understanding that is hard to describe in words. The best I can do is to compare the knowing sensation to having an intimate objective and subjective understanding of the topic from all conceivable perspectives. Simply: knowing.

All I had to do in the afterlife to explore a specific topic of interest was to focus my attention and intention on it. As soon as I intended to understand a subject, the knowing of it unfolded in my mind. It took no time at all for me to absorb the knowledge. More important, I remembered that I had known it all before I assumed human life. Though I had not realized it while in the body, the truth has always been there, all the time, accessible to anyone open to receiving it.

Other afterlife experiencers have also described the "knowing" sensation, acknowledging that they too recognized the information as it was received. For example, Virginia Rivers, in Dr. Kenneth Ring's book *Lessons From the Light*, recalled her NDE when she suffered a near-fatal pneumonia in 1986:

> As each second passed, there was more to learn, answers to questions, meanings and definitions, philosophies and reasons, histories, mysteries, and so much more, all pouring into my mind. I remember thinking, "I knew that, I know I did. Where has it all been?" . . .
>
> . . . Each passing second I was absorbing more and more

knowledge. No one spoke to me, nor did I hear voices in my head. The knowledge just seemed to "BE" and with each new awareness came a familiarity.[1]

Similarly, afterlife experiencer Beverly Brodsky related in the same book being inundated with remembered knowings, initially via telepathy from a Being of Light and later as direct infusions of knowledge. Ms. Brodsky had been raised with Jewish traditions but was a self-proclaimed atheist when she was injured in a motorcycle accident in her twenties. Though her body did not actually die, Beverly nevertheless left it and entered the Light. She remembers:

And within myself, as I was given the answer, my own awakening mind now responded in the same manner: "Of course," I would think, "I already know that. How could I ever have forgotten!"

In time the questions ceased, because I suddenly was filled with all the Being's wisdom. I was given more than just the answers to my questions; all knowledge unfolded to me, like the instant blossoming of an infinite number of flowers all at once. I was filled with God's knowledge.[2]

Betty Eadie, author of the best seller *Embraced by the Light*, relates being filled with truths during her afterlife experience, attributing them to God's Light:

Then questions began coming to my mind. I wanted to know why I had died as I had—not prematurely, but how my spirit had come to him before the resurrection. I was still laboring under the teachings and beliefs of my childhood. His light now began to fill my mind, and my questions were answered even before I fully asked them. His light was knowledge. It had power to fill me with all truth.

As I gained confidence and let the light flow into me, my questions came faster than I thought possible, and they were just as quickly answered. And the answers were absolute and complete. . . . This knowledge was more like remembering. Things were coming back to me from long before my life on earth, things that had been purposely blocked from me by a "veil" of forgetfulness at my birth.[3]

Mrs. Eadie, a high school graduate mother of seven, died at age thirty-one during surgery and returned. She is part Native American and was raised on a reservation and in Catholic boarding schools.

Reading these particular NDE accounts and others verified that the knowings I received were not unique to me. It also reinforced my conviction that knowledge obtained in the afterlife is true. The truth resonates deeply within us as we hear it. We remember this knowledge we held dear before entering into human life. Therefore, near-death and afterlife experiencers are my own personal ultimate authorities on eternal life topics, instead of religion.

My second step was to determine whether the truths about religious history that I observed in the afterlife documentary were already well known in the academic world. I thought it entirely possible that I was simply ignorant of changes in religious beliefs since my school days. Fortunately, I discovered the work of researcher and educator Richard Elliott Friedman.[4] Professor Friedman earned his doctoral degree at Harvard and was a Visiting Fellow at both Oxford and Cambridge—very impressive credentials.

Dr. Friedman's books introduced me to the world of biblical scholars, highly educated men and women who approach the Bible as a work of literature, rather than as an article of faith, and research its historical underpinnings. Some of them have written best sellers accessible to everyone in the years since I returned from the hereafter.

Reading these popular books opened my eyes to the fact that much of what I had seen in the afterlife documentary has become known to mankind since I died—at least to some. Obviously Source intends for this information to be disseminated for it is coming through in a variety of ways.

My science background convinces me it is important to use a logical methodology to assess the NDE and biblical research I collected if I want to use it to validate my own experience of history. I chose to adopt Dr. Friedman's description of how scholars approach studying religious literature as my framework:

> When a book is studied in a high school or university class, one usually learns something of the author's life, and generally this contributes to the understanding of the book.
>
> . . . If one is interested in the historicity of the biblical accounts, then one must inquire into when the writer lived. Was the writer a witness to the events he described? If not, what were his sources? What were his interests? Was the writer a priest or a lay person, a man or a woman, someone associated with the court or a commoner? Whom did he favor, whom did he oppose, from where did he come? And so on.[5]

This scholarly approach does not validate or invalidate the truth of the written word. It simply casts new light on the authors' language choices so that we can determine for ourselves how and whether personal backgrounds influenced their writings.

Applying Dr. Friedman's approach to the afterlife experiencer accounts I have read reveals that they have some advantages over scripture. Most of the NDE authors I cite are alive today and can be interviewed to test their memories and credibility. We have access to the educational, experiential, and religious backgrounds that provided the words and comparisons the NDE authors use to describe supernatural events that essentially cannot be accurately related in words. We can determine for ourselves what impact an author's background, interests, and religious beliefs may have had upon his or her rendering of the story. NDE authors can also be questioned directly about the meaning of their chosen terms and phrases, negating the need for individual or institutional interpretation of their writings. Finally, NDErs are not just eyewitnesses to the afterlife events they describe; they intimately experienced them.

Obviously, scripture was written thousands of years ago. The authors cannot be questioned about their backgrounds or meanings. In addition, scholars profess that the Torah and Bible were not written at the times of the events they describe. The sciences of carbon dating of parchment and ink, combined with textual criticism (the science of discerning the original words of a text from altered manuscripts), have allowed researchers to more nearly identify the origins of the oldest existing copies of these sacred works. The Torah, the first five books of the Old Testament, was compiled from pre-existing anonymous documents first composed between 922 B.C. and 587 B.C.[6] The New Testament Gospels date to between AD 70 and the second century.[7] These dates make it clear that scripture authors were not eyewitnesses to the events they recorded. More important, their original manuscripts have never been discovered.

We afterlife experiencers operate under a couple of unique handicaps when we try to relate the knowings that enlightened us. There are few human words and concepts available to communicate the true flavor and color of what we understood via telepathy. We often have to either invent our own vocabulary, or borrow words overloaded with unwanted meaning, to reduce our knowings to language. Much of the truth we received is so completely foreign to human life that it cannot be translated into human terms. Consequently, NDErs are forced to resort to well-worn metaphors and analogies that may imply more restrictive meanings than we intend. Each experiencer's honest attempt to put into words the glories of Universal Knowledge is hampered not only by the limitations of his or her language skills, but also by the breadth of human experience from which he or she can draw comparisons.

Some NDE accounts may reflect solely human perspective, rather than enlightenment, if resuscitation prevented the afterlife transition process from completely unfolding. I noticed that my interpretation of what was happening to me changed dramatically as I processed through the various stages of spiritual transformation. What felt true early in the experience seemed naïve as the perspective from which I understood the knowings shifted from that of the human known as Nanci to a spiritual perspective, and then to Source's own unique perspective.

Authors of ancient religious texts likewise operated under writing handicaps. Literacy was rare in antiquity. It was common at the time to copy text without vowels, punctuation, or capital letters. Later interpreters have had to fill in the vowels to create words from alphabet soup, so we cannot be certain we have received the writers' intended message. We will never know whether the original manuscripts were renderings of ancient folklore, records of insights from Universal Knowledge, or works of fiction. The original documents are long gone, their authors unknown.[8] We do know, however, that the writings that later became the Bible evolved over thousands of years, were compiled from numerous sources, and were not written by the authors whose names are attached to them. The Bible source material later suffered multiple intentional and unintentional revisions, and became translated and mistranslated from and to languages that do not share cultural concepts. Bart D. Ehrman, a Distinguished Professor and Chair of the Department of

Religious Studies at the University of North Carolina at Chapel Hill, summarizes the Bible's origins this way:

> Just as human scribes had copied, and changed, the texts of scripture, so too had human authors originally *written* the texts of scripture. This was a human book from beginning to end. It was written by different human authors at different times and in different places to address different needs. Many of these authors no doubt felt they were inspired by God to say what they did, but they had their own perspectives, their own beliefs, their own views, their own needs, their own desires, their own understandings, their own theologies; and these perspectives, beliefs, views, needs, desires, understandings, and theologies informed everything they said.[9]

Dr. Ehrman's insight was confirmed to me by the afterlife documentary I experienced. But I do not take his words to be criticism. An overriding principle I learned by dying is that all perspectives are valid, and true, for those who hold them. Being inside the human experience temporarily blinds us to anything beyond animal logic. Yet there is room for each of us to open our hearts and minds to greater truths—the truths of Universal Knowledge that come to us through "knowings."

Perhaps our revered scriptures and afterlife experiencer accounts share a core of truth that shines through the human perspectives and language limitations of their respective authors. I have concluded from my own attempts to gain spiritual peace that we need not discard precious religious beliefs to accept afterlife experiencers' reports. The two can be complementary. Our belief foundations may rest in childhood religious instruction, with upper floors constructed upon principles of Universal Knowledge brought back to us from the Light. Or, we can view our religions as providing elementary education but now we are ready for the more advanced information afterlife experiencers offer.

This book traces my personal efforts to reconcile my pre-death Roman Catholic religious beliefs, where possible, with the new truths I gained in the hereafter. To do this, I reveal the bits and pieces of religious history memories that survived my reentry into this human body, and compare those memories to the afterlife accounts and scholarly findings about ancient religious texts that have helped me harmonize my religious and spiritual backgrounds. I do not remember all of history. Nor do I presume to survey all NDE accounts or scholarly works. But, perhaps something in my journey will help you in your own quest to harmonize religion and spirituality.

2

Creation of the Universe

NOTHING IN THE UNIVERSE IS more wondrous than its origin. Few of us know the full story of Creation, much less the glories of its evolution. We resign ourselves to being unfulfilled by brief religious accounts of Earth's formation and scientific theories we barely understand. Religion and science present their views as mutually exclusive, separating our two major information sources like prizefighters facing off from opposite corners of the ring. Having twice watched the universe form during my afterlife experience, I am convinced that religion and science are not adversaries. Their theories must simply be stitched together to understand the tapestry of Creation.

An eternal, supernatural Creator is the origin of the "big bang" chain reaction that scientists believe gave rise to the universe of galaxies and fathomless space. We call that source by many names, including God, Allah, and the Supreme Being. The Creator I knew intimately in the afterlife has no name. The Beings of Light I met simply referred to "the rest of us" when they meant the Creator. So I adopted the name Source for God upon my return to human life because it sums up the Creator's nature.

Source is the font of all knowledge, emotions, thought, creativity, life, love and energy. It created this physical universe. But Source *is not a being*, as I was taught to believe. Source has no body or form. Nor is it even remotely human-like in appearance, though that image is entirely understandable considering that humans believe themselves to be the zenith of creation. In fact, the belief that Source must be like humans is so strong that newly arrived souls often perceive Source in the form of their preferred religious idol. Source's natural form, however, more closely resembles an immense field of intensely charged energy—Source Energy.

The first time I watched Source create the universe was during the opening scenes of the documentary-style vision that appeared in my mind in the later stages of my afterlife experience—after meeting my five Light Being eternal friends, my life review, remembering hundreds of other physical lives, and accessing Universal Knowledge to answer all my questions. By the time I saw the documentary my thinking had been freed from the human bias that physical life is real and that Earth is the center of the universe. I had transformed into what I call a Being of Light that regarded humankind from a more loving, yet more objective, arms-length position.

I do not today remember many details of this first replay of Creation, though I know I saw every single moment of it. What I do recall from the documentary is presented throughout in italics, including everything I remember seeing, feeling, and thinking at the time I watched Earth's history. Thoughts that occurred to me years later as I wrote this account are in regular typeface.

> *I see the galaxy we call the Milky Way and watch the planets of my solar system form. I am observing from an aerial view, as though I were flying high above our solar system but still within the galaxy. Rock, dust, and gases bombard one another into uneasy truces as stars and planets. I am surprised that Mars is a verdant, life-sustaining planet because I was taught that its atmosphere had been destroyed long before I lived on Earth as Nanci.*

I do not now remember the cause of Mars' destruction. I remember only that a once beautiful, living planet was reduced to a dustbowl over eons.

As my view circles around Earth's solar system, I count more planets in our sun's orbit than astronomers had identified by the time I died in 1994. Knowings explain that humans by nature believe their observations to be fact, admitting little possibility that truths might exist beyond their five senses. So scientists stopped considering that there might be more planets in their solar system long ago.

I watch planet Earth coalesce out of gases, dust, rock, and all manner of celestial ingredients to form a solid mass. The new planet flames hot and fiery for thousands to millions of years, though all this monumental change takes but a few seconds in the documentary. Then Earth cools and the formation of landmasses and oceans necessary for habitation begins.

Millions of plant and animal species gradually begin life on the previously barren planet, arising as though by magic from the raw chemical and biological building blocks that abound on earth. More complex animals evolve from less complicated ones. Eventually, I see the first human species develop from lower animal life-forms.

The second time I witnessed the universe's birth was during the unexpected culmination of my afterlife experience, when my Energy merged into Source's massive Energy field. My consciousness wafted through one startling revelation after another as I slowly commingled with layer upon layer of Source Energy until I all but dissolved, like a comet losing mass as it streaks across the sky.

Early in the merger process, I *reexperienced* Creation as I remembered it from when I was still one with Source—before Source conceived of me as a separate character/personality within its own consciousness. I witnessed the universe's conception from three distinct simultaneous viewpoints. I relived Creation as Source, feeling its emotions and intentions. I observed the events from a witness' perspective of loving detachment. And, I felt my own emotions as the truths I beheld crashed with my human beliefs like freight trains running toward each other on the same track. During the visual experience, knowings explained anything I did not understand, as well as how Source viewed what was happening. The knowings served the same purpose as subtitles in a foreign film.

I present my memories here in linear form though the thoughts and events described actually occurred simultaneously. Nothing was communicated in words—not even the knowings—so I have constructed a verbal framework as best I can. Source in particular does not think in words. It thinks in whole constructs, such as total experiences, global understandings, or complete ideas with intricate details. The effect on me of Source thinking was very much like the knowings sensation I felt frequently in the afterlife. Nonetheless, in order to convey the experience, I have assigned words to Source's state of mind and emotions. I have used brackets at the beginning of each section to identify the frame of reference I am presenting at the time.

[How I describe Source's state of mind prior to Creation, speaking from its perspective:] *I am alone. It has been wonderful delving into my exquisite talents and abilities, my emotions and senses, and my intellect. I love experiencing myself so much I want more and different sensations. I want to explore my creativity and imagination. I can imagine what "not alone" feels like and want to feel it deeply. I can imagine character and personality traits different than mine and I want to know what it feels like to relate in ways foreign to my innate nature. So I will manifest my imagination to create new experiences for myself in different environments.*

[How I felt being that close to our Creator:] *The sensation of Source focusing its considerable creative talents to envision what we call a physical matter realm is like being inside the center of a massive laser beam or concentrated energy ray of some type. I see and feel something like a blast of patterns—a matrix of colors and forms—emanating from Source that I cannot begin to describe. There are literally no human words that fit the powers and concepts flowing from Source in explosion upon explosion of creative Energy. Massive amounts of Source's consciousness and Energy are being redirected to the creation of a physical universe. I recognize the effort as manifesting because I engaged in it myself earlier in this afterlife experience. But Source does not think of it that way or use that term. Source simply wills, and so it is.*

[How I describe Source's creative intentions, speaking from its perspective:] *I intend a cohesive environment (a universe) to exist. It will eventually fold in upon itself and dissipate, at which time I may create another if it pleases me. But, for now, this universe will exist. This universe model pleases me. I extend my own Energy throughout this Creation to energize, empower and sustain it. I intend to hold it lovingly in place in my thoughts and experience its creative evolution.*

[My own thoughts while observing Creation:]
*I watch Source mold and craft Creation, thinking
each possible scenario through to its logical conclusion
before deciding upon a model for this universe. Source's
thoughts about the universe do not resemble what
humans see as physical matter. Source does not create
static places or things. Rather, Source conceives of the
mental and Energetic processes or laws of nature
necessary to continuously bring about the ever-changing
dream world it desires.*

*I understand now. Humans believe physical matter
is real, solid, and fixed in time and space because it
appears that way to human senses. But in reality, the
universe is contained entirely within Source's mind. It
is imagined. A thought process that never left Source.
Source's Energy never converted into physical matter that
exists completely outside of Source, like I always thought.
The universe is more like a dreamscape or virtual world
than a solid matter construction. Every particle of what
humans perceive to be physical matter resides lovingly
within its Creator's own intellect—in thoughts, memory,
imagination, and beliefs. The universe consists entirely
of mental Energy no matter how it appears to humans.
Physical matter is not real in the same sense that Source
is real. I am distressed that this truth about the universe
is hidden from us while we share humans' lives.*

[How I interpret Source's thoughts about
evolution, speaking from Source's perspective:] *I
design each thought of Energized physical matter to*

seek and combine with other thoughts to form larger Energy patterns like places, things, and beings. I intend those larger Energy patterns to likewise combine, split apart, and recombine over the course of their existence to generate new creations that I can experience. I implant an evolutionary mandate into every particle of Energy—a circular process of creation, life, and merging back into my core intellect.

[My own thoughts when I learned about the cyclical process:] *All physical matter has a life cycle. Humans recognize the life cycles of plants and animals because these are relatively short. A man can observe the birth and death of an animal within his own lifetime. But the fact that humans are not able to observe the recurring phases of stars and continents does not mean these entities do not have them.*

I understand now that Source built what we call life cycles into the universe so that each part will self-perpetuate until limited by the life cycles of the larger systems within which they exist. The plants and animals on Earth are self-perpetuating: they reproduce within the confines of the life cycles of the environments in which they live. For example, dinosaurs reproduced until Earth's environmental changes ended their life patterns. The limiting factor was Earth's weather.

It is the ebb and flow of this repeating process that gives rise to what humans call death, because, to them, part of the cycle looks like an end rather than a transmutation of Energy into a new form. But I see that there is no literal death in our universe.

[How I interpret Source's thoughts on evolution, speaking from Source's perspective:] *I intend that gases and other atomic particles explode and attract one another to form light-generating stars, and coalesce into gaseous planets, as I create processes that cause thought-particles of matter to attract and form temporary bonds, and then relatively permanent masses. As molecular cohesion evolves, I will it to produce living creatures to populate the worlds. These creatures will be varied, and will range in complexity from simple one-celled organisms to multi-system biological wonders. They will reproduce themselves in the same cyclical patterns apparent throughout the universe itself.*

[My own thoughts while watching how the universe was designed:] *As a former biology and chemistry student, I am fascinated by the fact that Source specifically designs what scientists call "laws," like the law of gravity. My science background led me to believe those laws are inherent in the nature of physical matter, rather than external to it. Yet I see that science is wrong.*

I am surprised to learn that Source does not create specific objects, like stars, plants, animals or humans. This comes as news to me as my religion taught me that God created the sun, moon, stars, landmasses and oceans in the forms I observed while I was the human named Nanci. But Source manifests no finished products at all; nothing is created in the form in which humans now see it. Source does not make man "on the seventh day" or at any other time. Rather, Source creates the inherent evolutionary processes that ultimately result in an ever-unfolding wealth of physical matter delights.

[My thoughts as I observe evolution at work:] *I watch biological beings and creatures evolve on nearly every planet as well as within non-solid environments. Contrary to popular human belief, most planets in the universe are populated by creatures of various types, many far more advanced than humans.*

As I relive Creation, viewing it through Source's loving intentions and feeling the thrill of Source's emotions, I marvel at the simplicity and complexity of the burgeoning universe. And I remember everything! For the first time in my life as Nanci, I understand how and why the universe is created. It is both evolution and Divine intelligent design.

My research located only a handful of afterlife experiencers who describe witnessing the birth of the universe or Earth. In *Embraced by the Light*, Betty Eadie describes Creation this way:

Why would anyone want to come here [Earth]? In answer, I *remembered* the creation of the earth. I actually experienced it as if it were being reenacted before my eyes.

All people as spirits in the pre-mortal world took part in the creation of the earth. We were thrilled to be part of it. We were with God, and we knew that he created us, that we were his very own children. . . . Each spirit who was to come to earth assisted in planning the conditions on earth, including the laws of mortality which would govern us. These included the laws of physics as we know them, the limitations of our bodies, and spiritual powers that we would be able to access. We assisted God in the development of plants and animal life that would be here. Everything was created of spirit matter before it was created physically—solar systems, suns, moons, stars, planets, life upon the planets, mountains, rivers, seas, etc. I saw this process, and then, to further understand it, I was told by the Savior that the spirit creation could be compared to one of our photographic prints; the spirit creation would be like a sharp, brilliant print, and the earth would be like its dark negative.[1]

Another afterlife experiencer, Mellen-Thomas Benedict, describes his view of creation in *Lessons from the Light*:

Eventually, I got the feeling that I was going through everything that had ever been. I was seeing it all—galaxies became little stars, and superclusters of galaxies, and worlds upon worlds, and energy realms—it was just an amazing sight to behold. And it felt like I was zooming somewhere but I really think it was my consciousness just expanding at such a rapid rate. And it happened so quickly but it was in such detail that there came another light right at me and when I hit *this* light, it was like [pause] I dissolved or something. And I understood at that moment that I passed the big bang. That was the first light ever and I went *through* the big bang. That's what happened. I went through that membrane into this— what I guess the ancients have called the Void. Suddenly I was in this void and I was aware of everything that had ever been created. It was like I was looking out of God's eyes. I had become God.[2]

Mr. Benedict had been very ill with an incurable inoperable brain tumor in 1982 when he died in his sleep, according to his at-home caregiver. He had attended Catholic boarding schools, was baptized into the Salvation Army religion as a child, a time when his stepfather was moved around from one military base to another, and did not consider himself religious when he died. He did, however, consider humans to be a cancer upon the earth. Mr. Benedict retired young from being a lighting/cameraman for feature films and was an impoverished self-employed stained-glass artist at the time of his NDE.

Of course, all these eyewitness accounts of Creation bear little resemblance to the stories commonly circulated through the major religions.

The book of Genesis includes two Earth Creation stories from different ancient sources and viewpoints, with no hint of the origins of the remainder of the universe. Modern biblical scholars now agree that several source manuscripts not included in the Torah or Bible formed the basis for both these literary works.

Through a painstaking examination and comparison of original and translated texts from later time periods, linguists have identified four still undiscovered ancient manuscripts that appear to have provided the material for the first five books of the Old Testament, including Genesis. Experts believe the J text (because the writer referred to God as Jehovah/Yahweh) and the E text (because the author used Elohim as God's name) were written between 1200 and 722 B.C. The largest source document concentrates on laws and priestly matters and so is called P for Priest. The fourth source book, the one from which Deuteronomy and the next six books of the Old Testament was taken, is called D. Biblical researchers believe an unknown Redactor, or editor, pieced together material from these source texts and others to construct parts of the Old Testament.

The first Genesis story dapples fleeting glimpses of creation of Earth's skies, its land and waters, and the sun and moon.[3] Vegetation was created first, then animals, followed later by man in the first version of earth chronology. This Creation narrative is part of the tradition recorded in the ancient P manuscript, which then made its way into the Old Testament via the Redactor.

The second Creation story in Genesis begins: "These are the generations of the heavens and of the earth when they were created."[4] The sequence of Creation is slightly different. Though the scene once again opens with the propagation of plants, man is created before other animals in this second account. The Garden of Eden appears only in the second description, and yet its existence is overwhelmingly accepted by the faithful. Scholars believe this second version of creation originated in the J manuscript, parts of which are sprinkled throughout the Torah and Bible.[5]

The Holy Qur'an reflects a brief Creation story similar to Genesis. It reads in part: "Surely your Lord is Allah, Who created the heavens and the earth in six periods of time, and . . . He throws the veil of night over the day, . . . and (He created) the sun and the moon and the stars."[6]

All these ancient scriptural Creation stories reflect the primitive human notion that man is the center of the universe, casting Earth's origin in the starring role with no regard for anything beyond the human experience. Creation is attributed to a Creator whose only interest seems to be mankind. Such a narrow focus makes perfect sense to a populace limited in beliefs to what they observe with five human senses. Today's believers mentally integrate what is now known of the vastness of the universe and its wealth of celestial bodies into personal interpretations of Genesis and the Qur'an, while preserving the core belief in a Creator.

The scientific-minded among us, on the other hand, refuse to acknowledge the Creator and discount religions' versions of the origin of the universe in favor of either a "big bang" theory or unknown forces generating a "unified field." That unknown force is not unknown to believers in God. Science's big bang may simply be another way to describe the Energy and power that accompanied Creation as I witnessed it. According to NDEr and researcher P.M.H. Atwater: "Creation's beginning may not have been so much a big bang or big blast as the bursting forth of a great thought that stirred."[7]

Those of us who have witnessed Creation firsthand understand Source to have employed the phenomenon of manifesting physical reality to create the universe.[8] That power is hinted at in the Bible's account, where God's spirit is said to have moved upon the face of Earth's waters and land formation accomplished through dramatic utterance of the words: "Let there be . . . ."[9] These words are certainly reminiscent of my experience of Source willing the universe into existence. Thus, the eternal truth of Creation as a manifestation by Source is tucked modestly within scripture.

My own and other afterlife experiencers' accounts of Creation combine both spiritual and scientific concepts into a comprehensible whole. Source imagined our universe in love and joy and manifested it into physical reality through an explosion of its creative thoughts and Energy. The big bang of Source Energy evolved in accordance with Divine intention, following the scientific principles Source established to govern the universe's life cycle and return to its originator.

3

Our True Origin

RELIGIOUS TEXTS SPEAK OF GOD creating man in the sincere belief that we are humans. Medicine regales us with details of sperm meeting egg and cell division—science's view of our origins. But both belief systems miss the mark. We are not really humans, as I discovered while witnessing our conception within Source's mind. While I was still engrossed in Creation reminiscences, memories of Source forming the identities we assume are human surfaced.

I distinctly remembered *being* Source as I designed the universe. Paradoxically, I also monitored Creation in real time as a fascinated spectator. Memory and the sensation of peeking into an unknown past co-existed without contradiction because we are capable of multiple simultaneous levels of awareness in our spiritual state. I have separated my global impressions of our origins into linear sequences in order to relate them here.

[Remembering the events from Source's perspective:]
My manifested universe is expanding and evolving as planned, forming objects and creatures of delightful diversity that will in turn evolve into new forms and species for me to experience.

As categories of creatures and objects become stable enough to withstand the Energy boost, I will project my consciousness into them to experience physical matter as they do. I will see, touch, smell, and taste matter as they do. Locate myself in time and space as they do. Limit myself to their sizes, shapes, senses, urges, biological processes, and "lives." It will be the most glorious adventure! So utterly thrilling to anticipate! Such varied sensations. So freeing. I will know my universe through emotions and physical sensations and not just imagination and intellect.

I will know firsthand the concept of separateness from me. I will feel what it is like not *to be me. To experience total ignorance of my own nature as I inhabit the creatures and objects. What a concept! To be able to get outside myself and look back at me as though I were a different entity. To know myself from an objective stance. What an unbelievably rich understanding this will give me. I must do it.*

Oh! Oh! I intend some of the creatures to have just enough self-awareness to know they are alive. To know they exist and follow a birth, life, death pattern. To know they are mortal. As they evolve, they may even become aware enough to sense me inside them.

Oh my, not only will I experience separateness from myself, but also relationships with *myself! I will engage in actual relationships within myself with the creature parts of me not knowing that they are me. I will fool myself! Conflicts between my innate nature and those of my imagined creatures could develop while I inhabit them. I could know an entirely different aspect of myself—how I react to the conflicts, how I resolve them, how they affect my emotions. Oh, how mind-expanding!*

How incredibly fascinating and exciting!

I will craft individual characters[1] within my consciousness and then mentally project those characters' identities and personalities into the creatures and objects to play the various life roles they offer. Limiting myself in the physical world to predefined character parameters will offer such different experiences. Each character I play will be unique. Each will exhibit some measure of my own innate nature, combined with varying degrees of imagined traits foreign to my nature.

Each character I play will participate in the further defining and refining of the universe. All will be co-creators within me of the developing physical worlds. Groups of them will maintain the continuity of the manifestations within the physical worlds that most interest them. The incorporation of their character traits and personalities into the co-creation will spice up my adventures in the physical realm.

Each of my mental characters will carve its own path through physical life displaying the innate traits and abilities I have designed for it. Each will respond to the universe in its own fabulously creative way from the viewpoint of whatever physical form it enters. My consciousness characters will each reincarnate over and over into many, many creatures and objects throughout the universe until all possible experiences consistent with that character's traits have been explored. Though I may repeat entering into certain categories of creatures and objects via my mental characters, such as having numerous human lifetimes, the "life" experiences will always be different because of the unique interplay among the innate traits of the creatures or objects inhabited, my characters' personalities, and the evolution of the manifested universe in general. My consciousness characters will thus change and grow—they will evolve— as the physical world experiences mold them.

When a particular character part of me has completed its evolutionary cycle through multiple physical lifetimes, the character will reawaken to the knowledge that it is I—that it is merely a part of my consciousness. I will thus bring into my core consciousness all the experiences I seek.

[My thoughts at the time:] *I now understand intellectually that all of physical Creation consists entirely of Source's thoughts—creative thoughts called manifestations. The universe is a manifestation both in the sense that it is a visible expression of Source's creativity and in the spiritual sense of being Source's inward imagination at work.*

I now remember that Source, as the only living entity in our universe, literally subdivides its consciousness into various characters to inhabit physical matter manifestations. But I find this nearly impossible to accept given the eons of living as a discrete being that I just remembered. It seems only seconds ago that memories of hundreds or thousands of physical lifetimes flooded my mind, each moment so crisp and clear that I marveled at how I could possibly have forgotten it. I know I am a separate identity from Source. I feel it. My sense of separation is real. I live my own life on my own terms. I am not perfect or Source-like by any stretch of the imagination. How could I be one of these Source characters in disguise?

Continued immersion in the memory of Creation helps convince me. I stare open-mouthed (as it were) as Source simultaneously and collectively through its imagined characters adopts the viewpoint and perspective of each manifestation and focuses part of its awareness upon what the creature or object is experiencing in the physical universe. It's all a matter of focus and intention for Source.

The process is somewhat similar to how I dreamt while inside Nanci. I was always both the dreamer and a character in the dream. I mentally created all the scenery (as Source created the universe) and the people (as Source manifested the creatures in the universe). I observed dreams from the visual perspective of one of the dream characters, usually one named Nanci, and adopted her viewpoint and role. In other words, I sat back and watched the dream unfold on its own through my dream character's eyes (just as Source allows its consciousness characters to create their own physical lives while it observes).

I now finally and deeply comprehend, and accept, that I am Source pretending to be someone other than the Almighty. I understand I was never actually human, as I thought I was while ensconced within Nanci's body. I now know that Source imagines characters, of which I am one, who then play various roles in the physical universe much like actors do in a movie. Human life is just *another role. All of what I always believed to be **my** life was actually just a role Source played as me. Wait—that means I am not **real**!*

*The ramifications of the revelation that I am not a real being careen about in my mind. Bone-crushing disillusionment chases wide-eyed wonder round and round for a hold on my heart. The shock would irreparably traumatize me were I not so totally intoxicated on Source's unconditional love. For a split-second I feel deceived. And I resent that I could not have been trusted with this knowledge before now. Am I but a toy to entertain Source? Has my physical and emotional pain been for naught—just to satisfy the curiosity of my Creator? These thoughts momentarily pierce my heart, counterbalanced by the truth that holds me firmly in Source's love: I **chose** this. I chose to share Nanci's life with her, including all her physical matter experiences—pain included. I did it to satisfy my **own** curiosity as Source.*

As Source? As Source?

*The greater truth starts to sink in. **I am Source**. I am the one who shaped part of my awareness and consciousness into the character that inhabited Nanci's body. I did this to myself!*

I have never been a separate being. Never separate from Source, from myself. Never alone out there in the universe. Although the identity I thought I had may not have been real, the painful illusion of isolation was not real either. Never alone. Never separate. Never unloved, no matter how it felt at times. Never alone or unloved . . .

because I am Source.

The truth is inescapable now that I know it.

The power of the truth, that the character I played is a beloved part of the God I had always worshiped, slams against my human religious background. Yet I feel awe beyond anything I ever knew in any physical life. Humility. Wonder. Mind-numbing humility. It's true. I know *it. I remember knowing this truth before I entered into Nanci's body. No choice not to believe it. The truth that I am God humbles me beyond my emotional capabilities. To accept that as Source I wanted to experience physical life as me. As* me*! That Source imagined* **me** *as a cherished character within itself.*

And I never knew it during human life. Never had a clue. Why had no one told me this? Why was it hidden from me? Surely someone *knew. Why did my religion lie to me about my very nature—claiming I am human and that Source is human-like as well? I know why, of course, because I just witnessed the history of religion and how it impacted all of mankind. But the raging unfairness is caught in my heart.*

Each of Source's excursions into physical matter experience engages a minute part of its awareness cast as a character that Source imagines, a limited role it plays. Each character is intentionally convinced that it exists separate and apart from the whole of Source—until it merges back into the whole. Yet a character is merely a set of real and imagined personality traits that Source combined to experience facets of the universe it cannot experience directly because of its immense size.

The complex personalities we ascribe to human beings actually belong to characters within Source's mind. I often call these characters "Beings of Light" because that is what near-death experiencers call them when they see Source's visual representations in the afterlife. Light Beings/Source's characters in their natural state "reside," for lack of a better word, in the afterlife. Actually, Light Beings are not "beings" at all. The "being" appearance, I discovered, disappears once the effects of human perception wear off in the afterlife—a state very few NDErs reach. Nor is the afterlife a "place" where one can reside. It is a state of awareness, existence, and perception.[2]

By re-experiencing Creation I remembered that **we** are those Light Beings. **We** are those characters Source created to play different roles. We are **not** the humans whose reflections we see in the mirror. Humans are manifested animals that inhabit planet Earth. Our relationship to them became clear as I merged further into Source's Energy corona:

> I see that Earth has captured my fellow Light Beings' interest early in its development. We observe with curiosity as the planet cools and becomes habitable. We Light Beings maintain our vigil as biological life emerges spontaneously on Earth, helped along by our co-creating, ultimately producing the upright walking animal that calls itself "human." Humans develop, as do all other earth life forms, through indigenous chemical and biological processes.
>
> I understand now that we characters within Source unknowingly reenact Creation every day in our "separate" lives, because we cannot help but do so. Creating is our innate nature because it is Source's innate nature. We are simply Source pretending to be separate beings. So, we too create roles to play as a way to experience and express

emotions that would not otherwise present themselves in our spiritual lives. But, at core, we remain ourselves.

We continue Source's work on a smaller scale by selecting creatures and objects in the universe, including human animals on Earth, to inhabit. Just as Source does not subdivide its entire consciousness into characters, we Light Being characters do not invest all of our Energy or consciousness into the physical world creature or object we inhabit. Part of us remains in the Light while one aspect of our multiple levels of awareness experiences physical life.

When we project part of what we believe to be our individual consciousness (which amounts to a yet smaller portion of Source's consciousness) into the perspectives of manifested beings and objects, humans call us "souls." We Light Being souls then "live" the various creatures' and objects' lives as roles in the manifested physical universe. A human animal, itself a manifestation, will live only one physical life. But for us, being inside a human is merely one of many roles we play.

For example, one Light Being inhabits Dustin Hoffman, sharing its personality and character traits with that human. One of the Light Being traits is the ability to change perspectives at will and portray another viewpoint, which makes Mr. Hoffman an excellent actor. He played the movie roles of Rainman and Tootsie with equal credibility. Dustin Hoffman invested himself in those roles and lived them fully, believably. Yet, he always knew that no matter how engrossed in the movie role he became, he was still Dustin Hoffman.

In the movie *Tootsie*, Dustin Hoffman mimicked Source even more fully than possible in most acting opportunities. Dustin played a man who impersonated a woman in order to get a job. Thus, he double role-played. Source likewise double role-plays. Source imagines characters within its consciousness (Beings of Light) who then imagine they play the role of human being. The Light Being and the human being each *know* for certain it exists, that it is alive, and that it is separate from the rest of Creation. Just as Source designed it!

Professional actors are not the only ones who reenact Creation over and over in their lives. We all do. Children play house, doctor, and space invaders just as they remember creating roles to play as Source. Teenagers may play the role of football hero, band nerd, femme fatale, geek, or other stereotype—roles that are dropped as soon as they get home to don the roles of younger brother, older sister, or only child, trying to behave as their parents expect. Many of us play roles in romantic relationships to win over a beloved. We act as we think our significant other wants us to act to earn their affection or attention. As adults, we role-play in our jobs. We say and do things that do not feel genuine because it is politically expedient and/or expected of us if we are to retain our positions. Some of us obviously role-play for a living, like actors, but writers, videogame creators, psychologists, lawyers, advertising executives and anyone else who must get into the mind set of other people to see as they see also role-play in order to accomplish a work goal. And we all dream. We pretend to do all kinds of things in our dreams, where we are safe from the consequences.

Most of us never realize we are Source pretending to be separate beings until we merge back into Source. We characters within Source's mind continue to believe we are separate individuals even in the afterlife—for as long as we desire and/or resist knowing that we are actually Source. Once we become aware we are Source literally playing a character, the façade of a separate identity dissolves. Maintaining the illusion of separateness requires ignorance of the magic behind it. Once we know the truth, we usually cannot forget it to continue playing the character.

Internet research led me to two other afterlife experience accounts relating to Source's creation of consciousness characters. Leonard, who provided no background beyond having died of a heart attack in the hospital, describes witnessing the event this way:

> Prior to universe creation there was only us, united in just one small point of awareness, this consciousness had knowledge but we could not experience it, then we separated into billions of individual consciousnesses and we created universe to go there and have fun! One day we shall all be reunited again, and again we shall "explode" and everything shall start again, this is an unending circle![3]

David Goines explains why we do not remember that we are characters within Source. A thirteen-year old David in extreme pain from five-way traction found himself in the Light after being hit by a concrete truck while riding his bicycle. Though not dead according to clinical standards, David nevertheless had a near-death experience. David's afterlife manifested as a heavenly garden. A kindly old gentleman sat down beside David on a marble bench in the garden to discuss life, death, and the afterlife as follows:

> I demanded of him: "How am I here, in this place, when I know that my body is back there in the hospital?" . . .
>
> He said, "It is your mental and spiritual body that is here. It is with your mental and spiritual eyes that you see this place. . . . This place is in your mind's eye, your imagination; it is as it is because this is exactly what you need it to be. . . . I am here for you on behalf of your heavenly Father's love for you

and to remind you from where you came."

My first thought was – The hospital?

He smiled a smile of wisdom and patience beyond wisdom itself and said lovingly, "No, I mean your Father's house."

It was then at that moment that I realized that I knew everything he was saying was true and that I had known this consciously before I was born to this Earth to have a physical body. I remembered that I was also a spiritual and mental body (being), and it all made perfect sense. I even remembered coming through the veil to find and choose my physical body. I was mildly puzzled that I could have even forgotten such things–when he reminded me that to have/ experience a physical life–it was necessary to at least for a while, forget a little of our prior knowledge so that we might more fully experience the physical things, be physically challenged, make choices of free agency, and yes, even make mistakes so that we could learn from them in ways that only a physical life could impart.[4]

Many religions teach that we are "children of God." The human parent-child concept is borrowed to give form and context to our innate intuition that we are part of Source. The construct is natural and logical for humans for no other physical bond connotes as high a degree of intimacy and love. The kernel of Universal Knowledge that we are part of Source is there. But it has been watered down to a human level that does more harm than good. The parent-child analogy figuratively cuts us off from Source. It casts us into separate beings essentially alone in the universe—just as human children are separate beings from their parents. That analogy not only fails to reflect our true nature, but also deceives us into believing we are powerless—like children. Nothing could be farther from the truth. We are, in fact, not Source's children. We are cherished, intimate, literal parts of its consciousness and self-awareness. We ARE Source.

4

No Warrior Angels, Devil or Hell

DURING MY CATHOLIC SCHOOL DAYS, I learned about angels who had warred for God's favor. The losing contingent, led by Archangel Lucifer, was cast out of heaven into a fiery abyss for all eternity. According to this legend, Lucifer, now called Satan or the Devil, roams the earth tempting humans into sin and damnation in order to increase his legions in hell.

Though I loved a good scary story as a child, I think the fallen angels tale is far too frightening for impressionable young children. I remember quaking in my little yellow rubber boots every time I ate a piece of candy that I had sworn to give up for Lent. I wondered whether Satan had tempted me, or if I truly wanted the candy. I imagined demons under my bed, waiting to snare my ankles come morning and drag me kicking and screaming down into hell. I went to Confession weekly to be purged of my soul-devouring sins of mean thoughts about another child or backtalking to my mother. I was nearly as consumed by fear for my soul's salvation as I was enamored with the medieval pageantry of the Catholic mass.

What a relief to learn in the afterlife that my childhood fears of the Devil were groundless. There are no fallen angels. In fact, there are no angels at all—at least not in the form portrayed by religions.

Before I died, I knew there was a widespread belief among Jews and Christians that Source created angels as a separate, higher level of beings than mankind.

Angels are allegedly pure spirits who can take on human bodies to enter the physical world. They are supposedly imbued with magical powers of upright bodily flight, the ability to work miracles, and freedom from physical incarnations. Angels are believed by humans to descend to earth to rescue us when spiritual frailty leaves us vulnerable to evil or misfortune.

I really want to meet those angels.

But watching Creation unfold, I see that Source does not fashion a separate and higher level of super-beings called angels. No heavenly choirs of winged majesty. No haloed miracle workers.

Knowings inform me that we Light Beings are actually the angels of human lore. When we leave this mortal realm, some of us serve Source and one another in roles that humans would ascribe to angels. Being an angel is a job, not a higher level of being. All the angel visitations and apparitions that humans report are glimpses of us Light Beings "on the job," as it were, either in our luminous state or in a manifested humanoid form donned specially for the occasion.

The replay of Creation during my merger into Source discloses no army of angels warring for Source's favor. No Michael the Archangel. No Angel Gabriel. No Lucifer. No loser angels are cast out into a fiery inferno, despite what my early religious instruction claimed.

Through benefit of knowings, I realize that the angel war story is human-created myth, projecting the human traits of competitiveness and jealousy onto imagined supernatural beings. The ancient story creates higher and lower levels of beings, which proves its human origin, for only animals have a concept of hierarchy. All of Source's creations are equal because they are all thoughts within Source's mind. Thoughts are inherently equal. One thought cannot outrank another. Equality reigns in our universe—creating hierarchies is a human pursuit.

Knowings I received earlier in my afterlife orientation are confirmed in this chapter of the memoirs of our universe's birth. Source does not create any type of opposite or adversary to befuddle men's minds or tempt mankind into forbidden pleasures. Nor does any evil being ever exist before or after creation of our Source-generated universe. Satan does not exist and never has. There is no role for the Devil to play. Humans are fully capable of all manner of evil on their own just by virtue of their innate cunning and violent nature. No outside force is necessary to spark evil. The Devil myth is part pure fearful imagination and part attempt to escape responsibility for human animal behavior ("The Devil made me do it!"). I learn that shirking responsibility for the consequences of one's own acts is an innately animal trait.

Nor did Source create a hell. There is no burning fire pit of pain and torment. No eternal prison where we are punished for acting like the human animals whose lives we came here to share. Remembering with Source, and as Source, the breadth and scope of the dramatically diverse wonders of this physical universe reassures me that there is no place on, above, or under the Earth like what we call Hell.

Granted, a few very prominent NDErs have reported seeing or entering hellish environments. For them, hell was real. I do not discount or disbelieve what they saw and felt. But other near-death experiencers report that we create our own hellish afterlife scenarios through the spiritual power of manifesting. The knowings these experiencers received detail how we are each capable of manifesting into reality our own hellish environments in both this life and the next.

The subject of hell was examined in depth during George Ritchie's NDE. Then a young soldier, George died of influenza in a military hospital in Abilene, Texas the day before he was scheduled to enroll in the University of Virginia medical school. Unaware of his clinical death, George rose out of his body and wandered off to find his clothes and duffel bag so he could catch the train to Virginia. He could not find his gear, and soon realized he could not find his body in the warren-like maze of hospital wards—because he did not recognize his own former physical host, which he had never seen in three dimensions! After finally identifying his body via a ring he recognized as his, George saw a man made of Light enter his room. The figure was accompanied by visions recounting every moment of George's twenty years of life.

After the life review, George and the Light Being flew high over Earth toward a distinct waterfront city that George took to be Boston or Detroit. As a spirit himself, George observed hundreds of other spirits invisible to the people in a factory they haunted. The spirits continued to try to perform their old jobs alongside their physical replacements. The invisible ones were dead but refused to accept it, and so they continued to live as they had while human. Later in his journey, at a large bar and grill near a naval base, George noticed that living people had a visible aura around them. The dead ones did not. George was amazed to see the envelope of light around a drunken man who had passed out split open at the top and peel off his body. One of the invisible dead seemed to jump inside the unconscious body in an effort to drink alcohol again. George tried to reason it out this way:

> Suppose that when they had been in these bodies they had developed a dependence on alcohol that went beyond the physical. That became mental. Spiritual, even. Then when they lost that body, except when they could briefly take possession of another one, they would be cut off for all eternity from the thing they could never stop craving.
>
> An eternity like that—the thought sent a chill shuddering through me—surely that would be a form of hell. I had always thought of hell, when I thought of it at all, as a fiery place somewhere beneath the earth where evil men like Hitler would burn forever. But what if one level of hell existed right here on the surface—unseen and unsuspected by the living people occupying the same space. What if it meant remaining on earth but never again able to make contact with it. . . . To want most, to burn with most desire, where you were most powerless—that would be hell indeed.
>
> Not "would be," I realized with a start. Was. This *was* hell: And I was as much a part of it as these other discarnate creatures. I had died. I had lost my physical body. I existed now in a realm that would not respond to me in any way.[1]

George and the Light Being continued onward to a barren plain where everyone was engaged in hand-to-hand fighting, cursing, and perversions of all kinds. No actual physical injury resulted because the combatants were already dead.

Now I saw that there were other kinds of chains. Here were no solid objects or people to enthrall the soul. These creatures seemed locked into habits of mind and emotion, into hatred, lust, destructive thought-patterns. . . .

And the thoughts most frequently communicated had to do with the superior knowledge, or abilities, or background of the thinker. "I told you so!" "I always knew!" "Didn't I warn you!" were shrieked into the echoing air over and over. With a feeling of sick familiarity I recognized here my own thinking. This was me, my very tone of voice—the righteous one, the award-winner, the churchgoer.[2]

As soon as George wondered why no one left this hellish place, which was not confined in any way, he noticed Beings of Light hovering above every single soul, ministering to him or her. He then realized he had seen the Light Beings in the factory and bar he had visited, but the invisible dead seemed to ignore their presence. George concluded: "Whether it was a physical appetite, an earthly concern, an absorption with self—whatever got in the way of His Light created the separation into which we stepped at death."[3]

Triple-afterlife experiencer Dannion Brinkley, author of the best-selling *Saved by the Light*[4] and founder of the Twilight Brigade/ Compassion in Action training program for hospice volunteers, quickly tunneled through what he calls a blue-gray place at the beginning of his first two NDEs. A lightening strike precipitated his first death as a twenty-five year old in 1975. Dannion returned to the afterlife during open-heart surgery. The third time, Dannion died of intracranial bleeding when an aneurysm ruptured during a flight from West Coast to East. This third time he stayed in the blue-gray place rather than speeding through it into the Light.

Dannion describes the blue-gray area as "the place where we can dwell as long as it takes for us to recognize ourselves as immortal spiritual beings rather than physical and mental beings."[5] He characterizes the blue-gray place as a supportive environment where we systematically shed our human characteristics and perspectives. I recall going through this shedding process early in my own afterlife experience, though the empty space I inhabited seemed whitish-golden to me.

Dannion observed miserable souls in the blue-gray place similar to those George Ritchie describes as occupying earth-like spiritual environments. He writes in *Secrets of the Light*:

Then I was abruptly overtaken by the uncomfortable presence of countless souls milling nearby. They seemed caught in a vicious repetition of recycled depression, dejection, and desperation. After a period of intense observation, I was suddenly impressed with the details of their stories. These souls were reliving their last days on Earth, over and over, without end. I was infused with the knowledge that some of these lost souls had been trapped in the heartbreaking shrine of emptiness, replaying the bleak misery of their lives for what felt like hundreds of years.[6]

Dannion observed in the blue-gray twilight many members of the military from all of Earth's wars, men who were unable to accept the extreme inhumanity in which they had participated. He also saw innocent war casualties trying to fathom how and why they had been killed. He could feel the emotions of victimized women from all walks of life and historical time periods. All these tortured souls continued their anguish into the afterlife. Dannion claims they were "all victims of a devastating absence of hope," who "lost sight of their self-respect, refused to express a genuine appreciation of life, or sacrificed the refuge of a meaningful spiritual foundation."[7]

Like Dr. Ritchie, Dannion Brinkley eventually understood that these souls in the blue-gray place "were not being detained against their will; they were held *by and according to* their will" and "only their inner light of hope, faith, and love could act to dispel the clouds casting the dark shadows over their self-imposed exile."[8]

These insightful hellish near-death experiences both confirm and disprove elements of the religious model of hell. The stories confirm that each of us has the potential for great suffering because we control the course of our own lives, now and in the hereafter. We will continue habitual painful human ways of thinking and living, human fear, and self-erected emotional prisons even after the bodies we inhabit are gone, unless we are willing to let go of human life and its trappings. We must turn our attention away from who we thought we were, and accept that life continues in a different form after death, in order to move on to the bliss of spiritual life.

But Ritchie's and Brinkley's NDE accounts also disprove the existence of eternal damnation. Both men observed opportunities galore for their fellow sufferers to shift their focus from their torment to the love emanating from the Light. Each occupant of a self-imposed hell had the choice to leave his/her agony by simply letting go of it. No hell observed by these messengers from beyond was eternal.

Notably absent from both accounts, and those of other NDErs who have experienced their own versions of hell, are descriptions of fiery pits of burning tar and similar medieval tortures. Also missing is the Satan character described in religious lore. None of us, myself included, had our fears of Satan's existence confirmed. How then did the belief in Satan arise?

"Satan fell to earth from the pages of the Bible. Or, more precisely,

Satan fell to earth from the religious imagination of the Jewish people in antiquity," write religious studies scholars T. J. Wray and Gregory Mobley in their book *The Birth of Satan: Tracing the Devil's Biblical Roots.*[9]

Scholars who study and teach the origins and history of the Bible most often attribute the development of a Satan figure in early Jewish religious literature to the triumph of monotheism. Prior to and at the time the Jewish people settled on Yahweh as their one and only god, the most prevalent form of religion was polytheism. Most cultures believed in many gods of various characters, powers, and temperaments. Most humans believed unhappy events in human life were directly attributable to a specific god's ill humor. A shift to believing in one god named Yahweh (and called other names as time has passed) created a practical, as well as conceptual, hurdle in the blame game.

> Thus, Satan begins to appear with more frequency in the Bible *after* the triumph of monotheism.
>
> To point toward one more conclusion, although it may be premature, the consolidation of all divine powers into Yhwh may have had an unexpected side effect. That is, before the adoption of monotheism, the misfortunes suffered in life were often blamed on other gods or evil forces. In a monotheistic system, however, Yhwh alone is responsible. Because Yhwh embodies both good and evil, it seems likely that many people find it difficult to embrace a deity that intentionally inflicts suffering.[10]

The conundrum that monotheism creates for humans who want someone to blame for their misfortunes is vividly presented by philosopher-writer Robert Wright in his comprehensive text *The*

Evolution of God:

It is sometimes said that the monotheistic thesis arose as a way to "make sense of" the catastrophe that had befallen Jerusalem. This is accurate but inadequate. Yes, religions have always addressed the question of why bad things happen, and yes, that is a question Israel's exilic intellectuals had plenty of cause to ponder, and yes, this pondering led eventually to monotheism. So, there is a sense in which, as some have said, exilic theology was a solution to the "problem of evil" or the "problem of suffering." But this sense is pretty misleading. After all, the "problem of evil" doesn't arise in acute form unless you believe in a single all-powerful and good God. Only if God is omnipotent does all human suffering become something he is choosing to tolerate, and only if he is wholly benevolent does this choice become something of a puzzle. And this kind of god, infinite in power and goodness, is exactly the kind of god that, so far as we can tell, didn't exist before the exile; this is the kind of god whose emergence during the exile we're trying to *explain.* Monotheism can't be the premise of the theological reflection that created it.[11]

The solution was to create Satan—albeit so gradually that no one can be accused of fraud in the endeavor. "Satan is the personification of the dark side of the God, that element within Yahweh which obstructs the good," writes Jeffrey Burton Russell in *The Devil: Perceptions of Evil from Antiquity to Primitive Christianity.*[12] Satan's evil character was embellished over the centuries with borrowings from other Middle Eastern religions. Later versions of the Old Testament simply removed any references to death and destruction attributable to Yahweh's wrath, replacing them with accusations that

Satan had performed the evil deeds.[13] English translators then took the liberty of substituting the name Satan whenever the original text mentioned an adversary or the Lord's anger. Satan was even recast in the role of serpent in the Garden of Eden story centuries after the original scroll of Genesis was first written.[14]

The concept of hell likewise evolved during post-exile Jewish history, reflecting the extraordinary influence that religions of neighboring nations had upon Judaism. Early Israelite religion maintained that the land of the dead was a dark subterranean place called Sheol where everyone ended up regardless of righteousness. As Jewish beliefs changed over the centuries of exposure to Egyptian mythology and Zoroastrianism, a new concept of judgment arose in which the outcome of life hinged on one's behavior. The word *hell* itself is an amalgam of early Jewish references to the Valley of Hinnom, whose Aramaic form is *Ge Henna*; the Greek god Hades; and the German underworld goddess Hel. The Valley of Hinnom was notorious in biblical times as the site outside the holy city of Jerusalem where trash was burned and polytheists sacrificed their children's lives to the gods.[15]

"The idea of 'hell' does not appear in the Bible until the New Testament. The actual word, however, never appears. . . . The earliest reference we have to the idea of hell in the Bible is found in the Gospel of Mark, written around 70 C.E."[16] The Book of Revelation, an imaginary adventure, is the primary source of modern assumptions about hell. Additional apocalyptic writings can be found outside scripture, boiling up a cauldron of nightmarish creations of hell that have endured over the ages.

Reliving Creation while merged within Source impressed upon me the breadth and depth of the influence of pure animal fear on mankind's spiritual perspective. It is easy to see now how raw fear, enhanced by the Source-originating imagination and creativity of Light Being souls inside humans, generated such far-fetched loathsome creations as Satan and hell. Fear is an animal's instinctive early warning system that survival is at stake. Humans believe from experience that fear speaks the truth because they have relied upon it for tens of thousands of years to survive the wilds of primitive life on Earth. A bone-deep trust in fear is largely responsible for ancient, fearful, primitive beliefs enduring until today.

When one combines innate fear with the certainty that all things human must likewise exist at the spiritual level, the result is an all-too-believable evil being residing in a fiery lair, a Satan who can be blamed for everything humans do not want to accept responsibility for doing to themselves. And one of the worst things humans do to themselves is believe their behavior can expel them from Source's mind and unconditional love.

5

Humans Get Souls

AFTER I WATCHED THE HUMAN species evolve from less complex animals, the Earth story documentary gushed at fire hose pace. Millions of years of Earth history preceded man's evolution, of course, but I was focused forward on how religions influenced human development.

> *Comparing the events unfolding before my spiritual eyes with my rudimentary recollections of world history makes it clear to me that a first human species emerged before the current second version. The human species evolved twice—independently. These early bipeds I am watching are not the humans of recorded history, though their appearance is quite similar.*

> *Abruptly I realize that the documentary is well into man's early days on a global scale but I have not seen Adam and Eve. I mentally rewind to where the Adam and Eve story of my religion should occur. I think maybe I overlooked it first time around. But on second viewing I still see no first man or first woman. Hundreds and thousands of humans evolve at the same time in different locations across the globe. There is no single human birthplace like the Garden of Eden. Of course, I had never believed the apple and snake part of the Adam and Eve story. Not even the Catholic Church*

claims snakes can talk. But I had thought there might be some kernel of truth in the tale. Now I see there is not. Instead of an Adam and Eve story, I witness the human species evolving spontaneously all over the planet, along with the other earth flora and fauna. I feel this is what Source intended.

I watch man's early days on Earth and his budding awareness of being alive. Males and females cower in fear over the implications of the changes from light to darkness, variations in the weather, and the uncertainty of daily survival. Their lack of control over the environment causes the skittish human animals tremendous anxiety. Genetic memory at this stage has passed on only survival skills and archetypal animal behaviors.

Tens of thousands of years pass as humans live purely animal lives. They do not seek to understand themselves, or life, because it is simply a given that they are born, live for a few years and die, ever following the cyclical pattern Source designed into them.

Early humans indeed look much like artists' renderings of Cro-Magnon man, which brings a smile to mind. Men live primal lives in lush jungles of unspoiled vegetation, any one of which some might easily call the Garden of Eden. I watch humans spend their days eating, sleeping, procreating, recreating, and otherwise living as all other animals do. Their needs are met the same way as their fellow earthlings, through operation of the Source-designed survival instinct. They scavenge for food, water, and shelter and move as herds from place to place in search of fresh pickings. Humans are aware they are alive—are self-aware—in much the same way as animal behaviorists today observe elephants or dolphins to have life-awareness.

Then, sometime during what is demarcated as the First Earth Epoch by a floating timeline above the documentary, a miraculous and wonderful thing happens. In biblical terms: "and man became a living soul."¹ For the first time, we Light Being co-Creators within Source choose to bestow a quantum leap in evolution upon human animals. We intentionally infuse humans with additional Energy to alter their genetic codes and boost their development. We then choose to literally inhabit humans by infusing parts of our own Energy and consciousness into many of them—the first implantation of what humans will come to call "souls." We Light Being characters within Source do this to further our plan to experience the physical universe.

Knowings assure me that Source never intended that we characters control human animals, or any other physical matter life-form into which we invest some of our Energy as souls. We are simply there—within physical matter, including humans—to observe and experience physical life. The manifested creatures and objects retain their unique character traits and identities. Souls coexist with their physical hosts, inhabiting the same matter, experiencing one life, and interacting with their hosts in a myriad of harmonious and dissonant ways.

Yet, the Light Beings I observe, who (like me) are interested in Earth, seem to tinker with not only the environment but with human lives. I watch as from time to time we infuse knowings directly into those parts of us inhabiting humans as souls in such a way that the Universal Knowledge will be available to humans. Examples of knowings intended to be available to humans over the ages float into my mind, including various scientific discoveries, medical intuition, and creative imaginings of the future and life on other planets.

Though I had been informed very early in my afterlife sojourn, and accepted the knowledge, I am only now coming to grips emotionally with the fact that I am one of those Light Beings involved in maintaining the Earth manifestation. I had invested part of my own self-awareness into the human named Nanci. The identity I knew for forty-three years as Nanci is actually a majestic part of Source that once inhabited the body left behind in the radiology procedure room. And everyone I knew in human life is the same—not really humans at all. The "soul" has nothing to do with human beings.

The history of soul implantation enthralls me even more now that I know I am part of it. It had never occurred to me before this afterlife history lesson that humans might have existed for hundreds, or even thousands, of years without "souls" inside them.

As I watch this slice of history I understand the Adam and Eve story as a metaphor, an analogy, created to describe events that are beyond human comprehension because they are well outside common human experience. Adam and Eve is not a metaphor for the origin of humankind. Rather, the story depicts the effect of the

infusion of Light Being souls on the already existing hu-
man race. Primitive humans logically interpreted soul
implantation as their species' origin because infusion
of Light Being souls did, in essence, blend animals and
spiritual beings into "human beings."

Before seeing this afterlife documentary, I had assumed the Adam and Eve story was a simple means of referring to the creation of the entire human race. "And the Lord God formed man of the dust of the ground, and breathed into his nostrils the breath of life."[2] I believed early storytellers used this verse from Genesis as a shorthand reference to the long process of evolution, not as a literal recipe for creating a Frankenstein out of dust and breath. A simplistic and unscientific interpretation of man's origin made perfect sense in the context of the primitive times in which the story was conceived. Imagine trying to explain the biological principles of evolution to people who thought the sun rising and setting was magic or the work of a temperamental Sun God. Today I read this Genesis verse as capturing the complex concept of soul implantation with the simple verb "breathed"—which is a colorful way to characterize Source's awareness entering into man via Light Being souls.

The Adam and Eve story appears in several chapters of the Holy Qur'an with slightly different wording that points more directly at soul infusion. "And certainly We created man of clay that gives forth sound, of black mud fashioned in shape. . . . So when I have made him complete and breathed into him of My spirit . . . ."[3] This brief description of man's creation suffices for the purpose originally intended—as background for the concept of what religions today call "intelligent design."[4] But Muhammed may have also been trying to convey the truth that Source's Light Beings entered into humans after the species was formed.

The effect of Light Beings inhabiting humans as souls is like a cartoon light bulb going on over their heads. A whole new level of awareness gleams in their animal eyes as the additional Energy inside raises human awareness higher than it has ever been. Huge quantities of information and intelligence suffuse humans' developing brains—downloads of knowings from Universal Knowledge. Humans begin to eat of the tree of knowledge, as it were, through their indwelling Light Being souls' innate access to Universal Knowledge.

I understand as I watch this part of the documentary that Source has always intended for the Light Beings within humans to continue to have free access to the enlightenment and knowledge available through Source. Only the knowledge of who and what they really are is to remain hidden—until the Light Beings complete their journeys through physical matter.

The Bible's Adam and Eve story nods agreement with this truth about access to Universal Knowledge in the following verse:

And out of the ground made the Lord God to grow every tree that is pleasant to the sight, and good for food; the tree of life also in the midst of the garden, and the tree of knowledge of good and evil.[5]

In this Genesis passage the symbol of a tree is used because it was a familiar source of food, shelter, shade and other survival essentials at the time the book of Genesis was written. "Tree" is a metaphor for abundant and easily accessed life-sustaining goods. And, in this part of the story we see that humans had easy access to their souls' self-awareness, the tree of life, and to Universal Knowledge, the tree of knowledge.

The "knowing" attributed to eating the forbidden fruit is gaining conscious access to the dual levels of awareness hinted at in the fig leaf story. The Bible tells us that after eating the fruit of the tree of knowledge Adam's and Eve's "eyes . . . were opened" and "they knew that they were naked."[6] Here the dual levels of awareness are identified as eyes opened, i.e., enlightenment of the soul, and awareness of nakedness, awareness of inhabiting the human body. The beauty of this part of Genesis is that ancient prophets were actually informing us of the truth of our dual natures—wisdom now ignored or misinterpreted by many.

The fact of human enlightenment is confirmed in the next verse when Adam and Eve hear "the voice of the Lord God," who is figuratively walking in the garden.[7] Communication with Source is not mentioned prior to eating the forbidden fruit, which stands for the infusion of souls.

Much later in the afterlife religious documentary, I observed that Catholic Church leaders who compiled the Bible revised the Adam and Eve story to add the prohibition against eating the fruit of the tree of knowledge, for the Church's control over members hinged in part upon its ability to prevent the faithful from accessing Universal Knowledge freely on their own. The serpent correctly informed the mythical Eve that knowledge would open their eyes and make them "as gods," for one of the fundamentals of Universal Knowledge is knowing that each of us is literally Source.

We Light Beings are part of one Collective Being I call Source. Therefore, we share the same innate characteristics. We have the same abilities as Source (though on a reduced basis because we are only parts of Source's consciousness). Having that knowledge could lead soul-infused humans away from organized religions to the serenity of higher levels of understanding on an individual basis. Growth of any unified religion would have been impossible if every member were free to believe his/her own individual truths. So the serpent was added to the fable to exert control over Jews, encouraging them to turn to religious leaders for instruction and away from their own internal access to eternal truths.

6

The First Humans' Beliefs

EARLY IN EARTH'S HISTORY, LIGHT Beings mired in mortal flesh did not suffer *total* amnesia regarding their true identity. Sparks of Universal Knowledge about Source and a life beyond the physical remembered by Light Being souls imbued the combined body/souls with self-awareness beyond that of human animals. Souls guided their host bodies toward religion and spirituality in an attempt to understand that glimmer of awareness of our true nature, and to reconcile flashes of enlightenment with the world of matter they encountered. The afterlife documentary showed me the simplistic ways the blended humans/souls devised to address the souls' primordial need to understand:

> *It occurs to me as I continue to watch First Epoch history that physical matter is far too dense and rudimentary to hold all the knowledge accessible to Light Beings. That, in part, causes the amnesia that prevents us from knowing our true nature while we inhabit humans. We cannot exercise our full mental capacities in human form, so it feels like our powers and knowledge as parts of Source are completely inaccessible. Knowings remind me that Source intends for its characters to suffer amnesia, because it makes the human experience seem real.*
>
> *I hear in these first humans the whispers of Light*

Beings within cautiously reminding themselves of a true nature barely remembered. This new, higher level of self-awareness frightens the primitive human hosts. We amnesiac souls inside are concurrently troubled by the nagging questions of how we got here—into the physical world—and what to do about our host bodies' consternation over being suddenly aware of their own existence.

I observe humans slowly develop religions as knowings inform me of how Source views their efforts. These early humans/souls find everything external to them wondrous and magical. They astound me with their apparent understanding that everything in nature is alive, including rocks, clouds, and the wind, though they do not know the source of that life. We souls inside cannot remember that the entire universe is composed of identical Source Energy, thought Energy. So only the barest concept of life filters through to the human mind. It translates into "Spirit." Early humans begin to believe that Spirit inhabits all of nature, including man, conferring life. The most basic of eternal truths is accepted and honored by creatures today's scientists would consider backwards.

The belief in one Spirit erodes over time. Human observation that each creature and object is distinct and separate taints spiritual truth to the point that a belief in multiple spirits emerges. Man accepts the new truth that different Spirits govern different living things.

It is a small jump from believing in multiple Spirits inhabiting nature to thinking that multiple gods control nature. I watch as humans project god-like status on many natural phenomena—wind storms, ocean tides, the earth movement that causes the sun and moon to seemingly rise and set, and star shine—simply through ignorance of science and awe of Mother Nature.

Each small cluster of humans crafts its own superstitions based on natural phenomena. According to human logic, the gods controlling the environment and its creatures must have the personalities reflected in their outward behaviors. Humans are self-absorbed by nature. So, as expected, they assume the gods must be motivated by the same drives and emotions man experiences.

I feel the unconditional love Source wraps around these flawed belief systems, partly because they are so human and consequently doomed to veer off into superstition. Source's lack of judgment resembles the same sense of tender observation a parent focuses on an infant exploring its new world while hindered by a lack of knowledge and experience.

Most of what happened during the First Earth Epoch, the millions of years before the current *Homo sapiens* species evolved, is lost to me now. As I was hurtling back toward reincarnating into this body, I tried to remember more, but I could retain only a brief overview of the time period that included dinosaurs and the proverbial Lost City of Atlantis:

I recognize glimmers of truth and understanding surfacing in the human population over tens of thousands of years. Humankind is slowly evolving. Humans' belief systems grow with them and diverge as groups separate.

Rudimentary forms of the sciences of medicine,

astronomy, and mathematics develop through Universal Knowledge infusions into Light Being souls. The ability to predict some natural phenomena, like phases of the moon, timing of tides, and weather patterns, partially satisfies our hosts' need for control and gives them the security required for complex civilizations to arise.

Mankind's focus shifts from survival to enjoyment of life. Formal religions sprout. Great cities are built. Life is sophisticated and rich at the end of the First Earth Epoch. Although I do not recognize any city like Atlantis, I note the existence of cities of its type, and of other now extinct highly developed cultures, just prior to the end of the First Epoch.

Then the planetary crust shifts. Earth tilts slightly on its axis, continents and oceans shift, and all manner of natural disasters wipe out most of life on Earth. The timeline at the top of the documentary discloses that I am witnessing the end of the First Earth Epoch, when evolved creatures like dinosaurs and humans are wiped out by tremendous planetary changes. Knowings indicate that all these changes conform to the life-cycle Source built into the planetary systems.

I regret I do not remember more about the first species of humans, or about the physical changes on earth that brought the First Epoch to such a dramatic halt. Other NDErs fill in some of the blanks in their accounts of history, but no one I located knew exactly what happed during the change in epochs.

Richard Langdon wrote to give me his very similar description of this time period, which he viewed as part of an afterlife historical documentary presented during his own NDE:

I saw a period in early Human history . . . during what you may call the "Early First Epoch" (pre-biblical by about 8-12 thousand years, by my interpretation of my NDE . . . where Mankind had faced a near extinction and survived by becoming small bands of extended families of "Wanderers" (my wording) that spread out from Central and Northern Africa into other parts of the world, encountering other earlier Human species and intermingling with them. I see this as also the era of the creation of the early "Earth Gods" (again, my wording), religious movements that spread out from the farthest reaches of Human expansion back to the heartland of Africa and the Mediterranean. I believe that some of our earliest myths regarding direct experiences with Humans and Earth-bound gods, Angels, Spirits, etc., (and also myths of Human/Animal hybrid demi-gods) stem from this era, as well; and that they were based upon the experiences of Humans with Beings Of Light who were "experimenting" with different ways of interacting with physical reality.[1]

The most fascinating element of Richard's account is the impact that the first humans' spiritual experiences had upon later religions. Clearly the Old Testament and book of Revelation in the New Testament culled ancient stories like these for inclusion in the cultural mythology of peoples who lived thousands of years later. And thus began our current religions' entrenchment in primitive mythology.

7

Gods of the Current Epoch

*T*HE RELIGIOUS HISTORY OF THE *current Earth epoch begins once again with the evolution of a primitive human species. It is not the same genus and species that evolved to such heights in the First Epoch. Evolution has been set back thousands of years, and a new human species arises, mutating slowly over generations from a less complex animal* (I don't remember which one). *I'm tickled to finally know why scientists cannot find the "missing link" in human development. My vertebrate anatomy professor's mind would be blown to know that the human species evolved twice independently. Who knew?*

Knowings whisper that genetic memory, and the persistence of all the Light Beings who are interested in Earth, bring humankind through evolutionary growth faster during the Second Epoch than in the first one. I see that Light Beings have been tinkering with human DNA again so that it will not take as long for these humans to evolve to the state of those destroyed at the turn of the Epoch. I recall that Source, through its Light Being co-creators, occasionally changes the manifestation of various parts of its universe.

The timeline graphic at the top of the documentary

screen in my mind discloses that the Second Epoch includes all of recorded human history to date. Anthropologists and scientists believe they are chronicling the entire history of their species. My biology degree certainly did not prepare me for the revelation that there was an entire Earth Epoch populated by humans prior to the current one.

Knowings I received when I first entered the Light informed me that humans, as a species, are not readily able to turn their attention inward to access the knowledge of souls inhabiting them. Most are completely unaware of us Light Beings within, much less that our knowledge exceeds that of humans. This truth is visually played out as I observe human/soul beings projecting their search outward to find something to explain who they are and why they exist. Humans, of course, have no interest in such things for they are mere manifestations. We souls inside, however, keenly seek an understanding we barely remember from before we inhabited humans— knowledge that hauntingly lurks just beyond our grasp, at the outermost edge of our consciousness. Because of the amnesia inherent in entering into physical matter, our efforts fall far short of truth. True understanding of the nature of our existence is beyond human experience, and therefore believed by most of us to be beyond the human/ soul's comprehension. I know this situation thrills Source, for part of its purpose in creating the physical universe is to experience what it is like not to have total self-awareness.

I see primitive man in this Epoch once again misperceiving the nature of the universe. He assumes he is the center of Creation, the most important creature, and the only intelligent one. Most clusters of humans believe Earth exists solely for their personal benefit. I now see in operation the truth about humans that was downloaded into my mind when I first entered the Light. Humans are completely self-centered and self-absorbed by nature, by design. So I cannot fault them for their tunnel vision. Their actions reflect their limited animal nature.

I observe with compassion that as humankind evolves, fear of uncontrollable natural forces drives men to desperate acts. These fears have to be conquered; human survival is at stake. I empathically sense humans' panic, their sense of hopelessness.

I am aware of one other afterlife account of part of this time period in history. In 1953, Guenter Wagner, an eleven year old German boy, was knocked unconscious while jumping down the basement stairs in his parents' home. After he came to, Guenter realized he was lying on the basement floor. Suddenly, he heard an extremely uncomfortable ringing noise often associated with dying. He then "oozed" out of his body. Guenter did not go directly into the Light. Instead, he appears to have wandered around in a gray area between life and death, eventually traveling bodiless around his home and then out into space.

Eventually, Guenter entered into the Light, only to discover himself completely alone there, just as I did. He soon heard two voices via mental telepathy urging him to return to his world. Later in the experience, Guenter says a Being of Light spoke with him man-to-man. The Being showed Guenter scenes of wars, a preview of his future as an adult, and a view of himself lying on a hospital bed being pushed down a corridor.

The Being at one point took Guenter back in time to the Stone Age. Guenter describes a family scene from that time:

I was looking down on a group of people, men and women, who were dressed in furs, sitting around a campfire. I could see a woman with her baby on her back, and a man who was standing in front of the group obviously making a speech. Another man stood a little apart. . . .

"Now we have proof [said the man in the scene]. You have just heard for yourselves. What we have been suspecting is true. He who took on the difficult task of making such a dangerous journey has just returned and confirmed our suspicion. They want to resist us. However, we will not put up with that. I have told you again and again. Now the time has come to fight them. We must not wait until they have become stronger. They are still weak now. It is true. Nevertheless, think of the future! We will have to attack them now."

He was addressing the group of people in a very impressive manner . . . But suddenly I heard this other man, who was standing apart, say:

"I am primarily a hunter and fight the animals. I am not going to fight weaklings who start running away the very moment they catch sight of us. Every hunter would hurt his pride and honor if he did such a thing. We hunters fight the animals, which are by far more dangerous. Many brave hunters have hurt themselves in their fights. Nevertheless, we are prepared and willing to take the risk because we are hunters. I will never fight those weaklings."[1]

The scenes began to move very quickly until Guenter was again able to recognize grasslands edged by a tall forest. He found himself in the middle of a small village, where he heard the voices of those the man in the first scene intended to fight:

> "We cannot run away forever. How many times did we have to run away? Many, many times! Such beasts! They come and destroy our village! And every time we run away. But not this time! This time we are going to stay! It cannot go on like that forever."

> I could feel fear and anxiety. . . . Some voices said:

> "They eat meat! Imagine that! Meat! In addition, they build huge fires in the prairie. They dance around the fires and bathe in blood. However, what remains the worst: They eat meat. The very thought of it! In the end, they are going to eat our flesh too."[2]

The Being of Light accompanying Guenter expressed great distress at the number of humans that would be killed as a result of scenes like the one just witnessed.

The afterlife experience significantly changed Guenter's life. Memories of the event tortured him for weeks before a Being of Light appeared and told him to forget the NDE. As an adult, Guenter turned away from spirituality and lost himself in alcohol. Then he saw a TV show on NDEs that validated his experience and restored his memories. He claims he was cured that night of alcoholism. Guenter nearly died in the mid-1980s from three suicide attempts and a ruptured stomach, but did not have another NDE.

> *The solution to human survival fear, I see, is to deify incomprehensible forces in an effort to both appease and control them. Humans create gods to explain the*

machinations of a hostile world. They do not believe their gods created the earth elements they inhabit. Rather, men and women think the elements themselves are gods. Gods of wind, rain, lightning, moon, sun, star constellations, planets, and other natural phenomena are given character traits and motivations based upon the only behaviors known to mankind—those of animals. This presumed understanding allows man to identify with and ultimately to manipulate the gods to get better results.

The gods are naively assumed to be as subject to ill humors and devious motivations as humans are. This personification instills mankind with the confidence to approach the gods in an effort to curry their favor. The gods are, after all, just like animals or humans, only more powerful. And, though the gods' actions might seem whimsical viewed from the human perspective, at least there remains a possibility of controlling them. Humans believe appealing to gods' egos with worship and sacrifices will change their moods because buttering someone up works with humans. They also think the gods find certain behaviors offensive, and so create a whole laundry list of prohibited acts based on child-like superstition. Hope of controlling the gods is the only peace humankind can find from the constant threats to survival.

My research unearthed an example of early religious beliefs about conduct offensive to the gods:

The Semang, faced with a violent thunderstorm and aware that it resulted from their having watched dogs mate or from some comparable infraction, would desperately try to make amends, gashing their shins, mixing the blood with water, tossing it in the relevant god's general direction, and yelling, "Stop! Stop!"[3]

While these beliefs may seem a little silly to us in the twenty-first century, are they really any different than offering little wafers and wine to the Creator in a medieval-style ceremony complete with music and incense? Or giving up candy for Lent?

> *Early Second Epoch belief systems have no morality component that I can discern. No code of conduct for how to treat one another No concern with death or the afterlife. Religion seems to revolve around man's relationship with nature and its gods. Believing in nature gods seems strange in light of modern science's explanations for so much of what early man assumed to be the work of ill-tempered gods. But watching mankind try to understand life and his own existence, and fail, reminds me how much love Source holds for its creations. For it takes tremendous love to allow a precious truth-seeker the freedom to fail. It would have been so much easier for Source to just outright tell souls inside humans the truth. To simply download to souls the truths they seek. To reverse the amnesia. To spare us souls the pain, anxiety, and longing we share with our human hosts. But that would have deprived humans, souls, and Source of the glory of the experience of being an ignorant, struggling human trying to find his rightful place in the universe.*
>
> *I see that over a span of centuries souls do collectively continue to raise human self-awareness and intelligence levels. Unfortunately, the kernel of truth that we are all*

One Being, that we are all connected to one another within Source, gets mistranslated as it is strained through the mesh of human fear.

Group worship develops under the belief that better control over the gods can be gained through quantity. Primitive humans find solace in being part of a crowd subject to the gods' moods. Surely, our forebears reason, each of us appears less of a target when camouflaged behind multitudes of other potential disaster victims. Yet, as misguided and illogical as that sounds to me today, I see that these ancestors carry within them the seeds of truth, in the souls' memories. Some souls are starting to remember that something greater than humans truly exists. A surety that there is more to life than survival is born. And the quest for reunification with that Greater Power begins.

The gods of the mid-Second Epoch are many and varied. Some resemble man, except for designated supernatural powers. Mankind begins telling tales of feats of the gods to younger generations. Tales of how the wind and sea gods defeated man in various endeavors. Tales of how man stood up to the gods in battles of wits. Stories of gods having sex with humans (because that's human nature) abound. Sons of gods roam the earth and claim special status. Giant gods are imagined. And always the gods are treated as part of the family of man, whether feared or revered. Sacrificing in deference to the gods' power is commonplace, for one never knows what might provoke or please a god.

There still do not appear to be any religious beliefs

GODS OF THE CURRENT EPOCH

per se, other than in the existence of the various gods. There are no doctrines or philosophies about life or how it should be lived.

Nor do I perceive any concern about an afterlife among early humans/souls. Most assume life continues after death, probably because of the spark of truth generated by the souls within the bodies. The afterlife is presumed to occur underground, rather than in anything resembling a heaven above the earth. All who die pass into the same afterlife, for there is no concept of tying good or bad behavior to the outcome of life in these religions. Apparently the Light Being souls are able to communicate at least this much truth to their human hosts.

Though humans are instinctively competitive, it does not occur to them to compete for the afterlife based on factors like quantity or quality of sacrifices to the gods. The gods are deemed to be creatures of the physical world, like man, with power over only some aspects of it. There is no concept of an all-powerful or Creator God at this point in the saga.

As time passes, and physical resources are taxed to their limits within known habitats, human behavior becomes more competitive. Intragroup violence erupts. The victorious stay within the established group. The losers are cast out into the wilderness as outsiders. Victory in local skirmishes breeds greed. Soon humans become conquerors, moving out of their previously defined territories to overtake the lands and resources of clans of strangers. More violence ensues.

The competitive spirit eventually reaches into the realm of the gods, and certain men start claiming special access to, and direction from, mankind's various gods. Thus the prototype of "priest" or "rabbi" appears.

An excellent survey of religion that includes the early Second Epoch time period in depth is Robert Wright's book, *The Evolution of God*. The author reviews an aspect of early religious practices that has obviously had a tremendous impact on the development of religion among humans: the spiritual leader, prophet, or guru. Mr. Wright's irreverent treatment of the subject nevertheless gets the point across:

> There is in the world today a great and mysterious force that shapes the fortunes of millions of people. It is called the stock market. There are people who claim to have special insights into this force. They are called stock analysts. Most of them have often been wrong about the market's future behavior, and many of them have been wrong most of the time. In fact, it's not clear that their advice is worth anything at all. Reputable economists have argued that you're better off picking stocks randomly than seeking guidance from stock analysts; either way it's the blind leading the blind, but in one case you don't have to pay a commission.
>
> Nevertheless, stock analysis is a profitable line of work, even for some manifestly inept practitioners. Why? Because whenever people sense the presence of a puzzling and momentous force, they want to believe there is a way to comprehend it. If you can convince them that you're the key to comprehension, you can reach great stature.
>
> This fact has deeply shaped the evolution of religion, and it seems to have done so since very near the beginning. Once

there was belief in the supernatural, there was a demand for people who claimed to fathom it. And, judging by observed hunter-gatherer societies, there was a supply to meet the demand. . . .

The shaman represents a crucial step in the emergence of organized religion. He (or she, sometimes) is the link between earliest religion—a fluid amalgam of beliefs about a fluid amalgam of spirits—and what religion came to be: a distinct body of belief and practice, kept in shape by an authoritative institution. The shaman is the first step toward an archbishop or an ayatollah.[4]

As time progresses, I realize huge temples are built to honor various gods, where daily rituals and sacrifices are conducted in an effort to secure the gods' favor. I am flabbergasted to know how and why the mysterious wonders of the world like the pyramids and Stonehenge are created.[5]

I see a stone temple built in alignment with the Sun God to whom it is dedicated. The construction offers a window through which the sun shines directly onto a sacred spot at certain times of the year. The human clan believes the window focuses or funnels the Sun God's powers through the portal designed for that purpose. The high priest of that temple promises believers that he can harness the god's power as it emanates from the heavens by directing it through the portal in a concentrated form, like a laser beam. All one has to do is stand on the sacred spot while the sun shines through the portal to be bathed in the god's favor and powers. Of course, there is a charge for this service and the elaborate ritual accompanying it! I note many other temples dedicated to other gods constructed in mathematical alignment with astronomical references for this same reason.

Over time religions become saturated with human character traits. Competition for the gods' favor. Priests' greed aroused by the accumulation of wealth sacrificed to the gods. Religious leaders' arrogance in assuming they control communication between gods and men. Even violence seeps into spirituality. Battles are waged in the name of a favored god, as though a god of wind, or the Sun God, cared what lands and resources particular humans secured. The gods become more like mascots of war than deities, with humans usurping more and more power through dominance over each other and the environment.

The replay of Earth's saga moves forward in time, showing me that, as history has taught us, religions in various forms abound throughout the known world. Each religion represents a group's attempts to meet several intuitive needs: to control the unknown to gain security, to honestly search for the meaning of life, and to give voice to the truths of life as known to man. But these religions are nothing like those that existed the day I died. The religions of this ancient era more closely resemble daily superstitious rituals than institutionalized philosophies.

This history lesson displays the obvious in ways I could never have appreciated while in human life because of my religious upbringing: religion is essentially a conglomerate of superstitions. The really sad thing is that this remains true today. Despite all of mankind's dramatic innovations in science, technology, mathematics, medicine and the arts, his spiritual beliefs have been cemented in place by fear. Mankind has not moved a nanometer forward in its collective spiritual life beyond the primitive Earth creatures I am watching. Yet, as sad as that makes me, part of me rejoices that the manifested world operates exactly as Source intended. Humans are meant to be primitive, and so they remain. Their unsophisticated religious practices reflect their animal nature, but I love them for that. I feel a parental connection to these silly creatures with their outlandish spiritual practices.

My afterlife documentary, the Guenter Wagner NDE account, and recorded religious history appear to be in harmony concerning the early days of the current epoch. And what stands out the most in all of them is that human animal character traits forged the foundations of religious practices. Mankind spent far less time trying to fathom the meaning and truths of life, death, and the afterlife than it did projecting a sense of self-importance onto the spiritual fabric of society. And how did Source view this development? With love. Pure love. Loving acceptance that souls inside humans were doing exactly as intended: they were living as human animals, experiencing human foibles and failures, evolving the species biologically—but with little dashes of "knowings" thrown in by Light Beings to improve the experience.

8

Old Testament Times

*M*Y INTEREST SWELLS AS HISTORY *races toward a period I know well from the Old Testament. Though I understood before I died that much of the Old Testament is myth and allegory, such as the stories of Lot turned into a pillar of salt and Jonah swallowed by a whale, I still believed that the general course of Jewish history had been accurately charted in the Bible. To my great disappointment, the documentary shows me this is not true. I see no Moses in the bulrushes. No Moses at all, in fact. There is no parting of the Red Sea, or epic trek from Egypt to the Promised Land. No battle of Jericho with the walls tumbling down. I recognize nothing during this era resembling familiar Old Testament stories.*

Instead, my spiritual viewing screen flashes thousands of images, scenes of small barbaric clans all over the planet battling to the death over lands and goods. Those in the Middle East are shabbily dressed in filthy cloths and skins, reminding me more of cavemen than the proud Jewish race of the Old Testament. I can either hear them speaking or I can peek into thousands of their mental monologues at the same time. And I understand it all simultaneously. Men are waging wars for access to material riches, and sometimes to defend the reputation of a favored god among a pantheon of gods.

I recognize many of the gods from earlier time periods, such as the Sun God and Goddess of Fertility honored since the dawn of the Second Epoch. Many different ethnic groups appear to share gods, calling them by different names. The groups I watch intently— those residing along the eastern Mediterranean Sea— all believe in a pantheon of gods, just as their forebears did. Many gods are still primarily humanoid, exhibiting easily identifiable human character flaws.

Some Old Testament era religions retain the ancient ways. They worship natural phenomena and give homage to the sun, moon, stars, planets, wind and other forces of nature. A variation on this belief system holds that the stars and planets are not themselves gods, but are inhabited by gods. Whereas earlier in the Epoch humans were convinced the gods controlled only natural phenomena, proponents of these developing religions sincerely believe that various star and planet gods influence human behavior.

I am impressed by the heroic extent to which some highly educated men go to prove the factual foundations of their beliefs. Budding scientific fields and mathematics are bent, shoved, and twisted in an effort to prove empirically the truth of religious tenets. For example, astronomy is used to validate the religion astrology, which professes that the gods inhabiting various planets and star constellations control events on Earth by streaming unseen particles toward the planet. Believers are also convinced that a baby's first breath of these particles establishes his/her personality for life. The ultimate result is the horoscope of twelve astrological signs that has endured to this day.

The idea of heavenly hosts arises during this segment of religious history. I see that organized religions now include many gods arranged hierarchically by degrees of power, similar to the organization of a human king's court. Different cultures call the head or king god of this court different names, but most identify one as the highest deity—such as Zeus, Yahweh, or Marduk. Lesser deities and spirits of various powers constitute a court or council to the main god and are referred to as "the heavenly hosts."

Religion has progressed from individual or group worship based on fear to following fairly well-established rules or practices that must be adhered to by the faithful. Although many of these practices are largely ceremonial, some hold a measure of practical wisdom. For example, a certain food might be taboo for religious reasons but scientifically should be avoided for health reasons. Some of the early Jewish dietary laws fall into this category.

Temples are still the centers of religious practices but they are no longer built to align with astronomical landmarks, like constellations of stars. Houses of worship take on more of a community function and protect the stockpiles of goods offered in ritual sacrifices. The ancient priest prototype evolves into a religious leader identified with, and often housed within, a temple. A new tendency to worship the leader in addition to the god he represents gradually develops, born of human instincts and transference. The messenger becomes more important than the religious message because humans prefer instant gratification, and, it is far easier to assess the impact of one's actions on a priest representing a god than the invisible god himself. I feel the priests bloat with pride and self-importance when lesser men revere them.

Spiritual traditions have been passed from generation to generation via oral storytelling, gaining flourishes and grandiosity along the way. These tales and institutionalized rituals and practices are among the first to now be preserved in writing. I am astonished by the lack of uniformity of early written language— not the hieroglyphs and other pictorial languages with which I am familiar—but the languages with alphabets of letters. Each author I observe seems to use his own version and style of characters for alphabet letters. It is very clear to me that no other person could possibly read the writing unless he already knows what it says. (I am reminded of my own terrible penmanship, which even I can't read after I've forgotten what I intended to write). I realize that much of what later becomes the Old Testament is being written in this nearly indecipherable personal script, which means that later translators will essentially have to guess at what is written, using their knowledge of the oral traditions as guides. My faith in the accuracy of the Old Testament is forever shattered.

While researching the origins of the Old Testament for this book, I found that academicians have already discovered much of what I learned in this part of my afterlife documentary. Scholars explain that the Old Testament is the cultural mythology of the Jewish people and not an historically accurate rendering. I use the word "mythology" here not to imply that the history is imagined, but as shorthand for an oral tradition that adds color, warmth, and character to the nuggets of actual history nestled within. For example, Americans hold to the myth that John Smith and Pocahontas enjoyed a Thanksgiving feast with North American Indians, and that George Washington chopped down a cherry tree and confessed his deed when caught. No one really knows if either event transpired. But the stories reflect the kernels of truth that a truce was reached between European settlers and Native Americans, and that George Washington was reputed to be an honest man.

The Battle of Jericho, for instance, is a tale about perseverance more than a city's actual history. Archeologists who explored the area around the ancient site of Jericho have concluded that it was never taken by force by the Israelites, as described in the Bible.[1] Indeed, some researchers postulate that the early Israelites had been living in the area for generations. They found no support for the story that they had wondered for forty years in the desert, to then be led to the Promised Land by Yahweh.[2]

My observation that early authors recorded ancient oral traditions is validated by scholarly research. Current academic thinking is that most of the scripture writers did not record events they had personally witnessed. Tradition holds that Moses wrote the Torah, which is primarily about Moses' life, and that he was therefore reporting eyewitness testimony. But scholars now agree that Moses could not have written any part of it, for the Torah appears to combine manuscripts from several unknown authors now referred to by the letters, J, E, P and D.[3] Biblical scholars likewise regard the remainder of the Old Testament as the work of various unknown authors. Professor Burton Mack explains in *Who Wrote the New Testament* that Jews had been reimagining their epic history for generations by the time the Old Testament was formally compiled.

Some scholars even question whether Moses the person existed at all, suggesting his name and identity is used as a literary fiction representing the Jewish people.[4] Muslim NDEr Azmina Suleman, however, saw Moses among the various Beings of Light who appeared to her in human form during her afterlife visit. He was accompanied by Noah, Jesus, Buddha, Lord Krishna, Lord Vishnu, Muhammad and many others regarded by humans as prophets.[5]

The dramatic rise in human population combined with civic organization in the first half of the Second Epoch clearly resulted in extensive humanizing of religions. The gods were portrayed to be no more than superhuman and were organized into bureaucracies. Focus shifted from gods controlling nature to gods controlling human behavior. And mankind started chronicling its history as it was affected by religious developments. Despite all they got wrong from a spiritual perspective, our ancestors kept alive the idea of an intimate relationship with a deity—the eternal truth that we travel a personal journey within Source.

9

Conception of a Creator God

MY AFTERLIFE REVIEW OF THE current Epoch's religious history so far revealed humankind's belief in, if not devotion to, multiple gods—different ones at different times. Although some groups of humans included a supreme god in their pantheon, most did not. Gods were gods, humans were humans, and the existence of one had little to do with the existence of the other. However, this situation eventually changed with the gradual emergence of a creator god.

To my surprise, the Jewish people I observe in the years we label as BC continue to worship many different gods. My Church taught that Jews accepted and worshiped the one true God, called Yahweh (and other names) in Old Testament times. But now I see that they did not always do so. The Israelites are adopting and worshiping gods of conquering foreign powers and adding them to an ever-expanding host of supernatural beings. Yahweh is just one of many gods during this time period. And the concept of Yahweh seems to graft together earlier versions of various other gods.

I am given to understand as I watch, that just as humans once created gods out of the sun, moon, wind, sea and other natural phenomena, they now conceive of a male creator god who is responsible for forming Earth and its inhabitants. This god is not necessarily considered by Jews to be above all the other gods. And, he is cast in the human image, as are most other gods. This creator god acts just like humans, except he is credited with having created the land and man. The gods residing in the sky are not deemed to be creations of the creator god. They exist independently.

At first, the creator god seems rather impotent compared to the nature gods, like those who control the weather. What, after all, can the creator god do to punish man? Uncreate the world? That doesn't seem plausible. So the creator god is believed to exist, but no one seems to be worshiping him or making sacrifices to him. I sense that humans are far more concerned about the rigors of daily life than how life itself was created.

Knowings reveal to me that the creator god does not assume much prominence until after Egyptian, Greek, and Roman scientific discoveries disprove the existence of some of the natural phenomena gods. Then all of the superstitions, sacrificial rituals, and worship previously attached to other gods are shifted to the creator god. He becomes all-powerful in that he can now give life or take it, and not just create Earth and its people. This new concept makes the creator god the most deadly of weapons to have on a country's side in war. And this god apparently loves war, according to what I see.

A 2008 Pew Forum survey disclosed that eighty-two percent of Americans believe in a creator god or some other form of singular universal spirit. The tenets of many religions profess the creator god to be almighty. In other words, he has all the power that humans are capable of imagining from their limited mortal perspective. The creator god grants life and death, knows all, sees all, resides everywhere at once, and lives forever. In addition, because this god created the universe, he retains the ability to change it to benefit or harm mankind. These attributes certainly apply to Source, as I came to know it during my afterlife experience. But not in the way humans currently believe.

Source is all-powerful because it is the only entity in this universe. It is an Energy source (hence the name). Source created our universe entirely in its own mind. All the physical matter we see with our eyes, and with microscopes and telescopes, is a manifestation of Source's imagination. Source used its infinite creativity to envision the landscape we perceive as our physical universe and everything in it. That vision, however, takes place within Source's thoughts. What we perceive to be physical matter does not exist independently or separately from Source.

Source has the power over life and death because its thoughts control the manifestation we call the physical realm. All living matter began life as thought. Source imagined a being, animal, plant, or thing and its existence commenced to evolve from Source Energy contemporaneously with Source's intention that it should have life. All physical matter is alive to exactly the same extent. Humans only recognize life in plants and animals. But those manifestations are no different in quality or composition from rocks, planets, or air. Plants and animals seem more alive to humans merely because the quality of their lives more closely resembles man's.

Source is all-knowing because the only intelligence that exists in our universe is Source's. It knows all there is to know, because all there is to know is what Source knows. No manifested being could know something of which Source is unaware, for the only intelligence invested into that being is what Source gave it.

Source is all-seeing because it can access any and all parts of its own mind, wherein the manifested universe plays out. Because all of Creation resides within Source's mind, Source can observe all it created simultaneously.

Source is present everywhere and always, though that is a human perspective. Humans think of the creator god as a multidimensional being that can be physically, though invisibly, present at all points in the universe. That perspective is backwards. Source is present everywhere because *everywhere* exists *within* Source. Instead of viewing Source as a being outside the universe looking in, we should envision the universe as inside Source looking out.

Source by definition must be almighty. We Light Beings are mere subsets of Source's thoughts. Our thoughts are not original. They arise solely within Source, no matter how separate we might believe ourselves to be. Neither humans nor Light Beings can possibly conceive of a power that Source does not already hold, for our thoughts are limited by its thoughts. Our imagination is a subset of Source's. We cannot possibly create something that Source cannot create, because our creative powers come from Source.

In other words, our concept of an almighty deity is a self-fulfilling prophecy. Humans worship the whole of which they are parts. They revere the collective without seeing that they are within that collective.

Mankind's religions have cast Source as an outsider so that it can be deified as gods have been for millennia. But Source is not an outsider. WE Light Beings are insiders because we are part of Source's consciousness!

10

New Testament Times

THE AFTERLIFE DOCUMENTARY IS NOW replaying a time period during which the Bible implies that the Hebrews uniformly practice Judaism. But I see groups of people adhering to all sorts of beliefs. Some Hebrews secretly espouse belief systems that are more spiritual and soul-centered than mainstream Judaism. Some continue to cling to the polytheistic ways of the past. Others seem to believe the world they know will end in their own lifetime. They believe the Messiah will come immediately and rescue them from Roman dominance. There appears to be no predominant faith, no homogeneity of dogma.

I scrutinize Middle East history around the time we call the first century AD with growing interest and anticipation. I want so much to witness the birth and life of Christ, to see for myself the events recorded in the New Testament. But I am disappointed. The most incredible revelation in this history of faith is what it so glaringly omits. The documentary timeline moves well past the first century before I realize I did not witness Jesus' lifetime. The only explanation I can imagine is that I tuned out for a moment during this portion of the replay of history. So I mentally rewind and refocus my attention. I concentrate harder to perceive any aspects of

Jesus' life about to play out before me.

There is nothing!

The life of Jesus of Nazareth does not appear.

The documentary shows no Jesus Christ as he is depicted in the New Testament. No virgin birth in a Bethlehem stable. No life of teaching disciples and performing miracles. No Jesus who molded twelve apostles into the core of a new church. No last supper. No crucifixion as depicted on the Shroud of Turin. No resurrection witnessed by Mary Magdalene. Nothing whatsoever appears from the life of Christ as it was described to me throughout sixteen years of Christian education.

The true-life events of a man named Jesus from Nazareth are not even a blip on the radar screen of this religious retrospective. Knowings that accompany the visual record force me to understand that whoever the real, historical Jesus might have been, he did not knowingly or intentionally start a religious movement. As a person, he was not important to religious history at all.

I do see several men wandering around proclaiming that the Kingdom of Yahweh is at hand. Their message is that Yahweh's kingdom is open to all Jews, not just the members of the educated, wealthy and ruling classes, which is traditional Jewish belief at the time. These prophets are considered heretics. But no one person appears in what we call the first century with the private or public life and background of Jesus Christ as detailed in the Gospels and Christian traditions.

There are in fact hundreds of men named Jesus, and I recognize pieces and parts of Jesus' biblical life story played out in the lives of men scattered across a couple hundred years of history. It is as though the Gospel writers combined parts of a lot of different life stories and attributed them all to one man.

Knowings confirm that the Christ story is an outgrowth of oral history, cultural traditions that include elements of the real lives of many people as well as the imagined lives of a few pagan gods. Knowings inform me that the original Gospels were edited and embellished later by Christian writers to recast Jesus in the mold of the Jewish Messiah foreshadowed in Hebrew lore. This was done to serve the interests of the Roman Catholic Church when it set out to define and delimit Christian religious dogma in what are now considered the AD 3rd and 4th centuries.

Learning that Source attaches no significance whatsoever to Jesus of Nazareth's actual human life fills me with an anger I did not think possible for a spiritual being. My anger is not directed at Source, of course. I feel duped by my former human religion teachers. I am humiliated that I followed a man-made messiah my whole life as Nanci. Now I understand how and why the Christ myth got started, yet I am still emotionally wounded to realize that it is just that—a myth. My unconditionally loving attitude toward humans temporarily evaporates because I feel they manipulated me to control my behavior. Part of me is shocked beyond rational comprehension, mentally distracted to the point that the documentary pauses for a while.

My NDE research located only one other person who during his afterlife experience traveled back in history to the time of Christ. The KGB assassinated Russian scientist George Rodonaia by twice running a car over him on a Moscow sidewalk. Dr. Rodonaia held a medical degree, worked as a research scientist, and was an avowed atheist at the time of his death. His body was pronounced dead by three distinguished physicians on Friday and stored frozen in a morgue until an autopsy could be performed on Monday. Dr. Rodonaia left his body and entered a profound darkness immediately after death—until a hallway opened onto a warm, comforting, peaceful Light. After some time, Dr. Rodonaia engaged in a life review, where he relived his human life all at once. He visited his lifeless former body in the morgue and reexperienced the car striking him. He reports that he could hear the thoughts of everyone involved in the accident.

Like me, Dr. Rodonaia realized that, in the afterlife, all he had to do was focus his attention and intention on a topic and information would instantly come to him. So he reexamined everything he had ever learned. One topic he reviewed was religion:

I felt it necessary to learn about the Bible and philosophy. You want, you receive. Think and it comes to you. So I participated, I went back and lived in the minds of Jesus and his disciples. I heard their conversations, experienced eating, passing wine, smells, tastes—yet I had no body. I was pure consciousness. If I didn't understand what was happening, an explanation would come. But no teacher spoke. I explored the Roman Empire, Babylon, the times of Noah and Abraham. Any era you can name, I went there.[1]

Unfortunately, this quotation contains all that Dr. Rodonaia ever publicly released about his visit with Jesus.

Much later, after returning to his body, Dr. Rodonaia felt the excruciating pain of the coroner cutting his chest open during an autopsy that was conducted *three days* after he died. He was back! As a direct result of this afterlife experience, Dr. Rodonaia entered a seminary where he obtained a doctorate in theology and became a Georgian Orthodox priest. He then earned another doctorate in neuropathology, claiming what he learned in the afterlife allowed him to make sense of both religion and science.

I personally know three NDErs who met with Jesus not as a religious figure, but as a relative who welcomed them to the afterlife. NDE researcher and author P.M.H. Atwater described her afterlife experience to the Virginia Beach affiliate of the International Association for Near-Death Studies on June 3, 2006. She stated that after her life review, she encountered several deceased relatives. One was a red-haired, blue-eyed Jesus, wearing a simple white tunic tied at the waist with rope. Mrs. Atwater, a devout Christian, exclaimed that she recognized Jesus as her brother and reminisced with him about their lives together on earth. She did not identify the historical period in which they were brother and sister. Mrs. Atwater explained that she felt no need to worship her brother, but rather, felt only gratitude for his actions on earth.

Australian multiple NDEr and medical intuitive Carmel Bell writes that she met Jesus during her first NDE, when she burned to death at age twelve. She recognized him at that time as her grandfather. Carmel encountered Jesus again as an adult during her fourth NDE and held extensive conversations with him (quoted in part in Chapter 11). As her book reveals, Carmel's first relationship to Jesus may be familial but she clearly regards him as a religious figure.

One of my readers informed me by e-mail that during her NDE

she recognized Jesus as one of her husbands from a previous life. She received knowings that the Light Being who inhabited the historical Jesus had reincarnated many times into human life, just like everyone else.

Jody A. Long, author and co-director of the Near-Death Experience Research Foundation (NDERF), conducted a survey among more than six hundred NDErs who submitted their accounts to NDERF to determine who meets us after death. She reports that although 70 percent of NDErs do encounter a being of some type during their experience, only 12.7 percent of those responding reported seeing Jesus.[2]

To clarify, I am not saying that Jesus of Nazareth never existed as a human. I did not *see* such a human in the afterlife documentary about how religion influenced human development. I surmise that that might be because his *actual* life events did nothing to further the history of religion among humans. We have no record of actual events. No one followed Jesus around recording what he said, as was the case with Muhammad. Nor did Peter, James, or any of the other presumed apostles commission anyone to write their memoirs of life with Jesus, or even to summarize his teachings. One would think that if Jesus founded a new religion, or a new school of thought, his "first pope" Peter would have documented everything his successor would need to know to continue the Christian religion. Yet no one has found any fragment of documentation of Jesus' religious precepts. Everything found to date was written decades after the Jesus timeframe.

New Testament scholars who believe in Jesus cannot be certain exactly what he preached because there are no records of it and no eyewitness accounts. Nevertheless, according to Professor Bart Ehrman in *Misquoting Jesus: The Story Behind Who Changed the Bible and Why*:

> Most scholars remain convinced that Jesus proclaimed the
> coming Kingdom of God, in which there would be no more
> injustice, suffering, or evil, in which all people, rich and poor,
> slave and free, men and women, would be on equal footing.[3]

The Kingdom of Yahweh concept was not an apocalyptic vision
or description of what awaits us in heaven. Jesus, and others who
proclaimed the belief, used the phrase as a call to political action—
to create a new society unburdened by Roman oppression. The
political flavor of Jesus' reported message jumps off the pages in a
New Testament edition in which words attributed to him are in red
typeface. Burton Mack, then Professor of early Christianity at the
School of Theology at Claremont, adds that Jesus "did not create a
social program for others to follow or a religion that invited others
to see him as a god."[4] This conclusion is consistent with what I saw
regarding the lack of dogma in early Christian groups. What attracted
Jews to Christian sects was their core belief in the imminence of the
Kingdom of Yahweh on earth. That gave them hope.

The life ascribed to Jesus in the New Testament is known not to
be an accurate portrayal, according to scholars who have published
since my NDE. They say very few of Jesus' followers had ever met
him, and, because the original Christians did not consider Jesus to
be either the Christ or the Jewish Messiah, his background was not
important enough to document. Jesus' life did not become important
until hundreds of years later, when enforcement of Constantine's
edict spread the Christian movement throughout the Roman Empire
to gentiles whose pagan gods had grandiose biographies. By then, the
lack of detail about Jesus' pedigree encouraged mythmaking so that
his credentials would compare favorably with those of other gods.

Scholars claim the organized Christian Church constructed Jesus' biography fifty to 150 years after the fact.

By accident, I discovered stories about other people or gods that sound very much like Jesus' life as presented in the Gospels. The first concerned another wandering preacher from Jesus' own time:

> Ever hear of Apollonius of Tyana? Like Jesus, he lived in the first century CE. According to stories later told by his devotees, he traveled with his disciples from town to town doing miracles: curing the lame and the blind, casting out demons. These powers emanated from his special access to the divine—he was the son of God, some said—as did his gift of prophecy. He preached that people should worry less about material comforts and more about the fates of their souls, and he espoused an ethic of sharing. He was persecuted by the Romans, and upon death he ascended to heaven. This imparted a nice symmetry to his life, since his birth had been miraculous in the first place; before he was born, his divinity had been proclaimed to his mother by a heavenly figure.[5]

The second story reflects more of the eternal nature of Christ after the Roman Catholic Church began congealing beliefs into dogma:

> Osiris, who had been a major god in Egypt for millennia, bore a striking resemblance to the Jesus described in the Nicene Creed. He inhabited the afterworld, and he judged the recently deceased, granting eternal life to those who believed in him and lived by his code.[6]

Jonathan Young, Founding Curator of the Joseph Campbell Archives adds a third story, from ancient China. In 3000 BC the god Huang

Di emerged from the belly of a flying dragon while the great star Chi shone more brilliantly in the sky. The god became man and united his people as the first (possibly mythical) emperor of China.[7]

The theme of an immaculate conception was a common one in Greco-Roman tradition, particularly for great political leaders.[8] Ancient Zoroastrianism similarly included a virgin-birth savior story:

> According to Zoroastrianism, the present age is a time of great crisis, but "Saviors will come from the seed of Zoroaster, and in the end, the great Savior" shall restore all goodness. One such savior, according to Zoroastrian teaching, will be born of a virgin, bring about the resurrection of the dead, and make humankind immortal. It is not difficult to see connections between the anticipated Zoroastrian savior and the Christian savior, Jesus.[9]

I have no way to verify whether or not these stories about others are woven into the biblical Christ life story. But they do show that details of the life of Christ could have originated in ancient tales of other gods and been interwoven with bits of other individuals' lives. If so, the story follows an age-old literary formula still in use today: mysterious birth, humble childhood, and heroic adult life in which the subject saves people and performs miracles. Sound familiar from present day books and movies?

Another mechanism explaining how unverified early life stories about Jesus appeared in the New Testament is called "literary construction." The Gospel of Luke, which scholars date to around seventy-five years after Jesus' time,[10] includes stories that for historical reasons could not possibly have happened in Jesus' life. One example is Jesus allegedly being thrown out of the synagogue at Nazareth for reading scripture and being chased up a hill so that the crowd might throw him off a cliff.[11] Archaeological diggings have proven Nazareth had no synagogue, and thus no rolls of scripture to be read. Nor does it have a cliff. Luke's presumption that a man from a peasant village could read, when the literacy rate in that part of the world is estimated by anthropologists to have been 5 percent, is likewise historically implausible.[12] John Dominic Crossan explains in *Excavating Jesus* that the Luke Gospel writer retrofitted Jesus with a past commensurate with the time period in which the author himself was writing: "That story is not only *in*, it is also *from* a later layer of the Jesus tradition. It is, in other words, an incident created by the evangelist Luke himself."[13]

According to some scholars, the Gospel of Matthew likewise takes creative license with the facts when it comes to Jesus' early life. "We conclude that Matthew himself created that fictional or parabolic account of the birth of Jesus, that he did it quite deliberately to make him a divinely destined fulfillment of Moses."[14]

The consensus among scholars appears to be that the Gospels are amalgamations of multiple layers of writings over a period of roughly sixty to seventy years after the presumed historical date of Jesus' death.[15] Some of Jesus' alleged sayings are attributed to a Common Sayings Tradition found in non-biblical sources like the Q Gospel, the Gospel of Thomas, and the Didache, and later incorporated into the New Testament.[16] According to scholars, the bulk of the remainder of the New Testament "turns out to be a very small selection of texts from a large body of literature produced by various communities during the first one hundred years. These New Testament texts were collected in the interest of a particular form of Christian congregation that emerged only by degrees through the second to fourth centuries."[17]

Although the New Testament is predominantly not composed

of eyewitness accounts,[18] one expert contends that: "Learned Jews, a few clearly from Bethsaida, Capernaum, or Jerusalem, claimed in the first century and even before 70 C.E.[19] that Jesus had said and done what is recorded in Mark and the earliest sections of Matthew, Luke, and John."[20] A few sayings and pronouncements attributed to Jesus are regarded as having been written during the AD 20s by a possible contemporary of Jesus.[21] At best, experts agree, some of Jesus' original thoughts and traditions may appear in the New Testament.[22]

Because nearly all of the biblical writers followed the common practice of attributing their works to known historical figures, their real identities are unknown. There does appear to be a theory supported by evidence that the New Testament authors' intent was to create and define a new school of thought using Jesus as the figurehead. That philosophy later evolved into the Christian religions.[23]

It seems reasonable to me to believe that a Jesus of Nazareth did actually exist, based on NDE accounts in which the experiencer encountered him as a family member (despite the fact that researchers and archaeologists can find no hard proof he lived). But I cannot give credence to the biblical life story. Mythmaking about the origins of Christianity began contemporaneously with the religion's spread. Researchers agree that an extant copy of Paul's first letter to the Thessalonians, which was written only about twenty years after Jesus' presumed death, appears to be authentic.[24] Though Paul never met Jesus, he comes across in that letter as aware of at least hearsay versions of Jesus' life story—including that he was killed by the Jews and resurrected. However, as later segments of my afterlife documentary disclose, Jesus the person was not important to the growth of the Christian churches—only the idea of him as a god was.

11

Jesus Cast as Messiah

A S I CONTINUE WATCHING THE review of religious history, some of the knowings I received about human nature at the beginning of my afterlife adventure are reinforced by what I see:

> *I note that humans' innate nature as herd animals, led by one or more alpha and beta males per herd, tremendously affects their religions. After the alpha secures his role as leader, most other humans defer to his judgment regardless of misgivings, suspicions, and contrary beliefs. Moreover, once secure in the anonymity of the herd, humans will collectively turn to the alpha for protection, even in derogation of their own sense of survival. They seem to turn their will over to the alpha and follow blindly, even unto death. The sense I have as this observation unfolds is that fear drives humans to trust their leader more than their own survival instincts and resources. In other words, a herd with an alpha expects a savior. The Messiah movement was born by infusing these human animal traits into religious traditions.*

The hope for a savior permeates the thousands of years we call BC, and consequently the Bible. The Jewish people, once a proud independent nation, had been subjugated for centuries by conquering foreigners and longed to return to political prominence. So they pinned their hopes on a future descendent of the House of David, a long-revered and highly mythologized early monarch. Human nature gave rise to the hope for a messiah—a strong king who would lead the Hebrews out of captivity and restore their sovereignty. Religion elevated that hope to expectation.

Jesus of Nazareth did not fit the Messiah mold. According to legend, his message, like that of others at the time, was that mankind should repent its wickedness and prepare for the coming of the Lord. He is represented to have believed that the Kingdom of Yahweh was to be instituted on earth during Jesus' own lifetime. When that did not happen, his followers were at a loss to justify their core belief.

Human nature is to resist admitting error. So Jesus' first followers recast him as a new species of messiah—a spiritual leader thrust into the role of alpha and charged with the obligation of securing everlasting life for his herd. For a human, the logic is inescapable: the same dynamics applicable to physical life must govern spiritual life. If the Kingdom of Yahweh did not materialize on Earth when Jesus said it would, it must exist in the afterlife. And an alpha male is required to protect the herd from the feared unknown hazards to a peaceful journey into that afterlife. This theory, more than any other, set the foundations for the various early Christian religions.

Biblical scholars detail evidence suggesting that the dogma of Jesus the Christ as the son of Yahweh, and part of a Holy Trinity, arose hundreds of years after the historical man lived. Early Christians debated whether Jesus was a mere mortal, or totally divine. At stake was the theory that Jesus was a messiah whose death had redeemed mankind from its sins. Clearly, a mere mortal could not accomplish such a supernatural feat. Unless he was God's *adopted* son, as some proposed based upon manuscripts circulated at the time.[1]

Of course, the information I was given in the afterlife makes this human vs. divine debate moot. *We* Light Being souls inside humans are divine. Hence, there is no need for a spiritual messiah. To understand this eternal truth, we must first understand what was impressed upon me at the outset of my afterlife experience: human beings die. Permanently. These bodies we inhabit do not have an afterlife. They will not enter heaven. There will be no resurrection of the body at the end of the world. The body's ultimate destiny is to return to pure Source Energy particles from which all physical manifestations are created. No savior, of human origin or otherwise, can clutch human animals from the jaws of death.

What so many of us call the "soul" is not part of a human being at all. Soul is part of our spiritual being, our Light Being Energy, and Source's own consciousness and self-awareness. We each invest part of our Light Being Energy/Source self-awareness ("soul") into a human animal host, while the rest of our Energy, personality, and beingness remains in the Light. The soul's fate is not now and never has been tied to that of the physical host. It remains an integral part of our Light Being Energy residing in a spiritual state, or realm, if you prefer. *Soul* is a level of awareness, or one perspective of a multiple level of awareness spiritual being.

No messiah is needed to guide soul Energy "back" to anywhere. It never left what we call "the Light" or the afterlife. Souls, again, are a level of consciousness, neither part of a human nor separate entities from the Light Being minds in which they originate. And, just as a human's unconscious cannot get up and leave the human brain of which is it a part, soul Energy cannot actually leave the Light Being of which it is a part. Consequently, there is no role for a redeemer of souls. All a human has to do is wake up to escape the unconscious condition. All souls have to do is wake up to their true identity to resume spiritual life. It is an inside job, a task suited solely to the soul itself. No outsider like a savior need apply.

We are not humans. The persons we believe ourselves to be, the personalities we hold dear, are purely spiritual in nature as characters within Source's mind. We cannot die. We do continue to live after our bodies have died, euphemistically calling that period of our existence the afterlife rather than just "life." We will enter the Light and "heaven" because that is our origin, our home, our natural state of being. The process is automatic and universal.

Medical Intuitive Carmel Bell reveals the following conversation about how we came to exist that she had with Jesus during her fourth near-death experience:

> "Are you the son of God, really?"
>
> "I am." Jesus said simply. "I am the 'child' of That Which Is. I am part of That Which Is."
>
> "Am I?"
>
> "You are also a part of That Which Is." I looked at Jesus quietly, waiting for more.
>
> "That Which Is," he continued "is billions of souls, all together. That Which Is *cannot* be one Being, one man, one woman, one child. That Which Is cannot be one. It is many. You are part of that many that has chosen to be separate from One. You also are not a man, nor a woman, but are both and neither. You are human and not human. Spirit and not spirit. You are part of that many that has chosen to be separate."
>
> "Does my being separate upset That Which Is?"
>
> "No. It does not. You have not left. You are not gone. You have separated just as a child separates from you. You are living your soul's desire and that makes That Which Is

content. In fact," Jesus continued his explanation, "You being separate helps That Which Is understand this Universe." Jesus indicated the space all around us.[2]

It is Source's innate nature that dictates that we evolve in our thinking until we realize and accept that we are literally Source's thoughts and imagination, mental characters representing fragments of its own consciousness and personality. Only fear-driven human minds, intrinsically designed to live in herds led by alpha males, could conceive of the need for an alpha-male messiah to lead them back to Source.

At least the eternal truth that we do return to Source is preserved in the various religions that profess to believe in saviors.

12

Early "Christian" Groups

MY ELEMENTARY SCHOOL RELIGION CLASSES featured Christian Church history as depicted in the Bible. Nuns taught me that Jesus of Nazareth was the Messiah anticipated throughout Jewish history, and that he founded the Roman Catholic Church as the "one true church" by appointing Peter as the first Pope. That the Church teaches this mistake is understandable, say the experts. "That is exactly what the centrist Christians of the fourth century intended."[1] But the biblical version is certainly not what I saw of Christian history in the afterlife documentary.

> *I watch the Hebrew religion splinter into adversarial factions during the early first century. Many small groups of Jews, who might be perceived as heretics to mainstream Judaism, meet to discuss rumors of other beliefs, including the idea that the Kingdom of Yahweh will replace the Roman Empire during their lifetime. The Jews have been expecting a political messiah for generations. Many envision the launch of Yahweh's kingdom on earth to be a political coup. Others think "thy kingdom come" spells the end of the physical world. Rampant fear permeates their anguished whispered discussions.*
>
> *Knowings inform me that the small groups that historians will eventually call the "Kingdom of Yahweh*

sect" will be considered to be followers of Jesus, though it appears to me that most of them have never heard of him. I see that politically and socially oppressed groups spring up spontaneously around the new message that the Kingdom of Yahweh will include all classes of Jews, not just the wealthy and influential. Jesus of Nazareth is not identified in these groups as a leader of the movement.

The Kingdom of Yahweh sect members do not communicate group-to-group like an organized church would. Nor do they appear to know about one another. I perceive no attempt to organize under a purported pope or otherwise. In short, I see no structured religious movement headed by the twelve apostles during or shortly after the years of Jesus lifetime, as I was taught in school. No appointment of Peter as first Pope. No unbroken line of popes from Peter down to the present. No central leader at all. I cannot even identify a cohesive core of Jesus followers still banded together after his death.

The early Kingdom of Yahweh followers hold to no central dogma other than a belief that Yahweh intends to assume political leadership of the Israelites. Those who have heard of Jesus of Nazareth do not, for example, conceive of him as anything other than a man. He is not believed to be a messiah, or the son of Yahweh, or to have any supernatural powers. Some groups may not have even heard Jesus' version of the Kingdom of Yahweh message. In short, these groups do not consider themselves to be Jesus followers any more than today's Republicans view themselves as Abraham Lincoln followers. They are simply Jews who believe they need to prepare for the imminent advent of the Kingdom of Yahweh.

Several decades pass after Jesus' presumed death before I witness the dramatic changes in philosophy that give birth to the Christian Church. Kingdom of Yahweh believers begin to attract converts outside Judaism. A church history and dogma are required in order to compete with myriad entrenched religions that are rich in tradition. Jesus of Nazareth is posthumously designated as the founder of the Christian religion, and a life history is constructed for him to rival those of pagan gods and Hebrew leaders. Jesus is declared to be the Son of Yahweh in the same way that kings and powerful political leaders of the time claim to be sons of gods.

The early Jesus groups do not agree on how many gods they worship. Some believe only in Yahweh. Others are certain there are at least two gods: the vengeful, warring Yahweh of Judaism, and the god of love and forgiveness preached by Paul and his followers. Still other early Christians remain polytheists, honoring the many gods of antiquity.

No one in the early Jesus or Christian movements is revealed to me as a messenger of the spiritual truths I rediscovered earlier in this afterlife transition. Rather, many men and women shine as beacons of the new monotheism, drawing followers of many diverse beliefs. The spark of truth that there is one Creator, to whom we owe our lives, thus surfaces in a uniquely human way.

I recently solicited NDE accounts that include glimpses into first century history from on-line near-death experience interest groups, but received nothing to include in this discussion. So few NDErs have encountered historical visions in the afterlife that the lack of afterlife material on the early Christian era is not surprising.

The disjointed origin of Christianity I observed is well known to those who have studied this period. Historians are uncertain how many different philosophies and sects considered themselves to be followers of Jesus during the decades after his death. There were Jewish Christians, Ebionites, Nazareans, Gnostics, and others. Different writers have identified and named groups the Q Community, the Jesus School, the True Disciples, the Congregation of Israel, the Congregations of the Christ, and the Jerusalem Pillars, based upon each group's writings and how they referred to one other.

Scholars presume there was a group of Galileans headed by Peter formed during or shortly after the life of Jesus, though that does not comport with what I witnessed. If indeed there was a group of apostles, they left no written records intended as guidance for the new church. We know of the apostles' existence only from brief references in Paul's letter to the Galatians written around AD 55, one of the few epistles attributed to Paul that scholars believe to be authentic. In that letter, Paul mentions two trips to Jerusalem to visit the "pillars," identified as Peter, James (the brother of Jesus), and John, to discuss whether gentiles should be accepted into the Kingdom of Yahweh movement and, if so, whether they must be circumcised. The pillars' overall response to Paul's requests for guidance appears to be a hands-off attitude. Any idea that Peter was the first pope, and that he ran the original Catholic Church, is contradicted by the fact that he abdicated all authority over the gentile Christian groups to Paul. Moreover, experts agree that no other documents surviving from this time period mention Peter as the leader of the Kingdom of Yahweh movement, or refer to the so-called pillars at all.

Research confirms that many different groups coalesced around various understandings of the Kingdom of Yahweh message during the first forty years of the first century—the time when Jesus is believed to have lived. None considered Jesus to be the Messiah, risen or otherwise. None thought of themselves as Christians. They were exactly what I saw: Jews who believed that the Kingdom of Yahweh was right around the corner. We know this from a scholarly recreation of the writings of one group that date from the AD 20s to the Roman-Jewish War in the late sixties. The Sayings Gospel Q, as these writings are called, constitutes the earliest "Christian" documents available and is considered to be as close to what the historical Jesus may have taught as we will ever get. Even this material, however, was later edited to change Jesus' early teachings to bring them more in line with later developments in the new religion, resulting in Q^1 being considered the original, and Q^2 and Q^3 to be layers of subsequent revisions. According to Burton Mack, who has studied the texts in detail:

> The earliest layer, Q^1, consists largely of sayings about the wisdom of being a true follower of Jesus. Q^2, on the other hand, introduces prophetic and apocalyptic pronouncements of judgment upon those who refused to listen to the Jesus people. And Q^3 registers a retreat from the fray of public encounter to entertain thoughts of patience and piety for the enlightened ones while they wait for their moment of glory in some future time at the end of human history.[2]

The Q material most closely dated to the time of Jesus teaches that the Kingdom of Yahweh will belong to the poor, hungry and grieving. It admonishes that one should treat others as he/she would want to be treated (the Golden Rule), refrain from judging others, work to promote the Kingdom of Yahweh, ask for God the Father's help, and give up all material possessions. The Sayings Gospel Q declares that the Kingdom of Yahweh will exist on Earth by the end of the writers' own lifetime, and failure to take the Kingdom seriously will result in punishment. No biography is given for Jesus in it.

The revisions that gave rise to Q^2 appear to have been made in the AD 50s and 60s, after the Jesus followers had been persecuted for some time, say experts. The tone turns dark and threatening. Non-believers in the Kingdom of Yahweh are believed to be doomed. And, because the Kingdom obviously did not materialize before Jesus died, the conclusion was drawn that its realization was postponed until final judgment at the end of the world. The presumed original Jesus sayings were rewritten decades after his death to make them sound as though he had pronounced them with the judgment day flavor the editors added. More important, Jesus himself was recharacterized from wisdom teacher to apocalyptic prophet predicting what would happen at the end of the world, when in fact the Kingdom of Yahweh movement was founded on the premise that Yahweh would rule Israel in the early first century.

The third layer of Q revisions was added after the Roman-Jewish War of AD 66-70. By that time, Jesus had once again been upgraded—this time from prophet status to divine being. According to scholars, the third Sayings Gospel Q revision formed the basis for the New Testament Gospels of Matthew and Luke, written sometime after the early seventies. Consequently, those Gospels reflect more of what the Q Community later came to believe than Jesus' actual life and teachings. As time passed, more and more new material was written without regard to the facts of the historical Jesus and his presumed teachings. Burton Mack, Professor of early Christianity, suggests that the Christian movement took on a life of its own in a way that allowed it to compete with pagan beliefs and win converts, incorporating elements of Greco-Roman philosophy along the way:

The Q Community started with memories of Jesus as a Cynic-like sage, found it helpful to expand that to the role of a prophet, then further enhanced that role in order to account for all the knowledge being attributed to him. They ended by thinking of him as the envoy of divine wisdom and the son of God, two roles that had the effect of turning the historical teacher into the appearance of a divine being and his teachings into a revelation of cosmic arrangements. Before they were finished, the Q people had positioned themselves toward the end of a sweeping view of history from its beginning at the creation of the world to its ending with a judgment scene in which either God or Jesus would use the Book of Q as the standard for admission to the final form and manifestation of the kingdom of God.[3]

Obviously many of the Q material concepts are familiar to us, as they were absorbed into Christianity in its infancy.

The Gospel of Thomas, from the Nag Hammadi Library, is a Coptic translation from the original Greek manuscript of alleged Jesus' sayings similar to the first layer of the Sayings Gospel Q. The original Gospel of Thomas dates to AD 75-100, many decades after Jesus' death, and thus may or may not have a historical basis. The Gospel of Thomas reflects a sect of early Christians who did not take up the apocalyptic leanings of the Q Community. Nor did they adhere to the traditions of the Jewish-Christian groups. Like the Sayings Gospel Q, the Gospel of Thomas contains no biographical information about Jesus. Nothing is mentioned about Jesus' death, much less a dramatic death by crucifixion after betrayal by an apostle. These earliest writings by Jesus people demonstrate that in the beginning people followed the message rather than the messenger, adding new material and attributing it to their founder, as was the custom. The actual life and times of Jesus were not considered important because he was acknowledged to be a human wisdom teacher rather than a deity.

According to historians, the many and varied early Christian groups developed independently and created individualized belief systems. Later versions of Christianity all claimed to be Jesus' teachings because the tradition among writers at the time was to attribute later developments in philosoophy to the founder of the school rather than to the successors who conceived of them. Professor Burton Mack explains the genesis of these differing beliefs: "the different views and practices that developed are evidence for the fact that Jesus did not provide a program for starting a new religion. If he did, his followers did not understand what it was."[4]

Not only the Jesus teachings but also the portrayal of Jesus changed over time, creating an image far different than the man's actual life. The most profound development in early Christianity turned what started as the Kingdom of Yahweh movement into a cult of a god called Jesus Christ. When it became obvious in the first century that Yahweh was not going to establish an earthly kingdom, Jesus followers were left with a religion based upon a disproven fact. Rather than abandon the Kingdom of Yahweh belief entirely, the faithful reinterpreted it to mean that believers would enter into the Kingdom upon death. Jesus' death therefore took on tremendous significance. The fact that no one in the new movement knew the actual facts of his death allowed followers to create a new death story, one that portrayed Jesus as a martyr for his beliefs. We know this from the letters of Paul, which are the first documents to refer to Jesus by the Greek name Christos.

Scholars indirectly confirm my observation that Jesus did not start the Catholic religion. That was the role of an educated Jew named Paul, a Pharisee who once condemned followers of Jesus as Jewish heretics and then adopted his own beliefs about Jesus being the Christ. Experts agree that Paul was instrumental in bringing about the religion now called Christianity. His role was to organize cells of non-Jewish believers in each foreign city he visited on business. Paul's authentic letters, and those posthumously attributed to him, constitute over half of the New Testament. Experts say Paul's thinking and teachings, rather than those of Jesus, dominated the Christian Church as it spread among the gentiles. Paul admits he never met Jesus. Never heard him speak. He had only hearsay and rumors upon which to base his decision to expand the Jesus movement. Interestingly, scholars comment that Paul's view of Christianity did not match those of the other early Jesus-follower sects—particularly Paul's emphasis on love.

Paul, not Jesus, thus founded the traditional Christian religion, concludes scriptural studies expert Robert Price. This conclusion mirrors what I observed. Professor Price reports that the New Testament compilers attempted to represent the twelve Apostles' influence as equal to Paul's by adding the Acts of the Apostles to the canon "to imply that the Twelve had played some prominent role. If they ever had, their labors were among Jewish Christians in Palestine and largely forgotten after 70 AD/CE and the destruction of Jerusalem."[5] Professor Price adds: "It may attest the relative unimportance of the Twelve that no one made any attempt to even ascribe apostolic names to Mark's and Luke's narratives. . . . It is interesting that the two most common male names in the Roman Empire happened to be Mark and Luke."[6]

I learned through my afterlife experience that, contrary to my church's claim, Christian dogma and teachings were not channeled to humans from Yahweh, God, or Source. They have human fingerprints all over them. And that is just fine with Source. We Light Beings came here to experience what it is like to be human—including their belief systems, however they originated.

13

The Christian Church Organizes

ONCE GENTILES BEGAN CONVERTING TO the Kingdom of Yahweh sect, it mushroomed into a religious movement that spread throughout the Middle East. Different schools of Christian thought vied for the largest membership until, eventually, a catholic (in the sense of universal) or centrist Christian religion was organized using various versions of a bible as its charter.

I continue to watch religious history in the afterlife documentary intent upon learning the origins of my own religion, Roman Catholicism, or Christianity in general, for it is clear from what I have witnessed so far that Jesus of Nazareth did not establish the Catholic Church—or any other church.

I see men who were once certain that many human-like gods engineered, and interfered with, their lives begin to accept the message that an Israeli creator god is the most powerful. The truth of Source's existence nestled deep within Light Being souls confirms this core tenet of monotheism and encourages adherence to it. But the promising start on the road to truth is soon mired in the muck of human animal traits.

Spokesmen vie for leadership in the new faith with the same gusto as an animal feeding frenzy. Men adopt titles to elevate themselves above others in the

Christian community rather than emulate the humility of their avowed founder. Self-appointed bishops assume financial, ritual, and philosophical control over large geographic areas. Christian groups start to resemble exclusive cliques, complete with entry requirements like circumcision or renunciation of Judaism and all other belief systems.

The leadership contests spawn literature as each candidate for office records his own beliefs and interpretations of what the Kingdom of Yahweh stands for and against. Many, many epistles, gospels, and other texts are created and circulated. Some are a good-faith attempt to document honest beliefs about Jesus' teachings. Others represent religious beliefs cast as political platforms for which the candidate seeks support, with no effort made to maintain continuity with the Kingdom of Yahweh message. Many of these writings seamlessly blend age-old myth and tradition about other gods with Judaism and use it to create from whole cloth a new Christian tradition.

Over decades and centuries, conflicts develop between believers of one Christian tradition versus another. The debates are fueled by the fact that the movement chose a figurehead founder, Jesus of Nazareth, about whom almost nothing is known. He wrote nothing. His life and times were not recorded contemporaneously with his life, or later on by anyone who had known him personally. The man Jesus is not mentioned in the original version of any preserved historical record. No attempt was made to maintain his childhood home or the sites of his miracles. Nothing was done to preserve anything that might provide verifiable evidence of his Kingdom of Yahweh message. So any and all beliefs are fair game for the new religion. Heretics abound.

To my horror, I witness the founders of the Catholic Church changing the manuscripts that will ultimately make up the Christian Bible. Some parts are rewritten in order to make the revered writings say what Church fathers want followers to believe, to prevent what they deem to be heretical interpretations.

As I continue heavy-heartedly to watch the history of my religion play out on my mental view screen, it becomes clear that the Catholic Church is intentionally rewriting much of its early history and spiritual tradition for many different reasons. One is to subjugate women. Women were a driving force in the early days of the Christian movement, a role that threatens the male dominance instinct of Church fathers of this time period.

For example, the Adam and Eve story originally spoke of "man" as meaning the human race, including both sexes. I watch the Church fathers rewrite the story. By using a narrower interpretation of the word "man" Eve is demoted to a literal appendage of Adam and made out to be the villain in the biblical story of human origins.

My initial reaction to seeing the Church fathers deliberately demean women in their literature was to assume that I had interpreted history through the lens of my own belief in the equality of the sexes. I have found no NDE accounts on this point. But one biblical scholar published an opinion that supports my memory on this facet of the documentary:

Scribes who were not altogether satisfied with what the New Testament books said modified their words to make them more clearly support orthodox Christianity and more vigorously oppose heretics, women, Jews, and pagans.[1]

Bart Ehrman attributes this grafting of the predominant bigoted attitude toward women onto Jesus' message to Paul's failure to clearly preserve respect for women in his letters to the early Christian churches.[2] Later on, scribes simply edited Paul's epistles to suppress the role of women in the Church forever.

Bible researchers I have read have independently come to believe what I concluded while watching the afterlife documentary: Christianity was not founded upon the actual life or teachings of Jesus of Nazareth. The Christian Church rests upon pillars of thought constructed decades to centuries after the events allegedly memorialized in the Gospels.

The four Gospels of the New Testament have been dated to writings from no earlier than AD 70 (Jesus of Nazareth is believed to have died in AD 30-33) to as late as the second century.[3] Neither Jesus' disciples nor anyone else who might personally know his life story could have authored them. "For more than two hundred years most New Testament experts have concluded that the Evangelists [Matthew, Mark, Luke and John] did not know the historical Jesus; moreover, they wrote decades after his death. . . . The Evangelists were not eyewitnesses of Jesus' life and thought."[4] Therefore they could not have authoritatively written his life story.

The authors of Matthew and Luke "also felt free to change Jesus traditions, including altering words attributed to Jesus," and "sometimes significantly and deliberately edited Jesus' sayings," states internationally recognized expert James H. Charlesworth, Director of the Princeton Theological Seminary Dead Sea Scrolls Project.[5] This scholarly deduction comports with what I saw in the documentary of early Church officials writing down their own beliefs about Jesus and Christianity.

Biblical scholars similarly confirm what I saw about Bible text being changed over time by Church founders. Professor Bart Ehrman's *Misquoting Jesus: The Story Behind Who Changed the Bible and Why* details the hundreds of thousands of copying mistakes, mistranslations, and intentional editorial changes, that have crept into various versions of the Bible. He identifies some of the changes as intended to solidify the orthodox Catholic Church's teachings and prevent scripture from being used to support other Christian traditions.[6]

Many more changes were simple copying errors made when scribes, often illiterate, hand-copied texts. The original Greek manuscripts that formed the New Testament were written in a style that used no spaces between words or sentences, no punctuation, no capital letters, and no paragraph or verse indications.[7] Scribes who copied them added their own word and sentence structure. More devastating to the accuracy of later translations, early scribes used no vowels and often abbreviated words to save space in scripture.[8] So educated guesses have been made at what scripture authors originally wrote in a process more difficult than guessing the missing letters on TV's *Wheel of Fortune*.

The Bible, it turns out, is not a textbook of God's Law, as I was taught in Catholic schools. Source did not command any one person or group of people, to sit down and record instructions to mankind. The Bible is not that type of testament. The New Testament in particular is simply a pick-and-choose collection of Christian writings that were popular from roughly a hundred to four hundred years after the death of Christ. Robert Price, who has studied and written about fifty-four Christian texts excluded from the New Testament says: "The selection of the books for the canon was gradual and to some degree haphazard. It was the result of a gradual accumulation of local usage and then a comparison of such local versions and usages by larger councils."[9] None of the individual texts was penned for the purpose of inclusion in the Bible. Nor was any book known to be authored for the purpose of conveying Christ's words. In fact, one can easily tell how little of the New Testament is actually attributed to Christ speaking in those Bible editions in which Jesus' words are printed in red.

Early Christian historian Burton Mack explains that the New Testament, despite its questionable origins, was nevertheless compiled as a charter for institutionalizing the Christian Church:

> The problem is that this charter was created for the fourth-century church by means of literary fictions. It is neither an authentic account of Christian beginnings nor an accurate rehearsal of the history of the empire church. Historians of religion would call it myth.[10]

Yet the Bible did accomplish its intended mission of providing Christianity with the credentials needed to expand throughout Constantine's Roman Empire.

Bible scholar confirmation of various afterlife documentary events resolved much of the conflict I felt between what I had seen in the afterlife and what I had been taught in religion classes. I now understand that the various texts of scripture record human beliefs, hopes, and insights in an attempt to create a united Christian Church that could withstand attacks from outsiders at a time when Christians were persecuted for their beliefs. Christian leaders were not trying to deceive anyone, least of all their followers. Everyone did what he thought was best for the Christian Church and for the salvation of mankind in general. Human nature got in the way, as it often does, resulting in the usual competitiveness, violence, and mythmaking taking its toll on religion the same way it does in secular life.

14

Christianity Spreads

THE EMOTIONAL SHOCK OF LEARNING that the roots of the religion that guided my life for forty-three years differed radically from what I had been taught prevented me from focusing on the details of Christianity's development after Emperor Constantine's reign. I regret that now. I have always loved to read about medieval times, with its castles, moats, and bawdy culture, and wish I had perked up and paid attention when that time period played out before me. I also wish I could remember more details of earlier time periods in history. What I remember now are simply overall impressions I formed of Christianity's tortured evolution over two millennia.

> *Like all human endeavors, Christianity organizes into a hierarchy as it grows. I watch as leadership is centered in Rome until the Catholic Church splits along political lines into eastern and western churches.*

> *Knowings inform me as I witness religious history through the first and second millennia that some organized religions fall into the trap of devoting more effort to controlling human behavior than seeking to know Source. They do not realize they are doing this, of course, for they believe in good faith that strict adherence to ancient religious teachings holds the key to salvation. Human fear blinds them to the truth that all of creation*

is part of Source and therefore automatically returns to Source. Salvation is inherent in the nature of creation and does not have to be earned—through faith, good works, or sacrifice.

In some eras I see men seize upon institutionalized religion to serve their own human animal needs. Human nature includes a competitiveness that drives men to attempt to dominate others. Churches are attractive to unscrupulous Alpha males because they represent amassed populations that might be easily dominated and manipulated through fear. Certain men assume power as church leaders and blatantly preach that they control access to God and entry into the afterlife. This gives them a false sense of tremendous power. But it is very effective with the faithful.

Think about it. Does not a man who claims to know how best to please your Maker, the Supreme Being, who theoretically can smite you down at any moment, have tremendous power over you? James Redfield, author of the modern-day parable *The Celestine Prophecy* described this emotional hold well when he wrote the following:

"Okay," he [character Wayne Dobson, NYU history professor] replied, "imagine yourself being alive in the year one thousand, in what we have called the Middle Ages. The first thing you must understand is that the reality of this time is being defined by the powerful churchmen of the Christian church. Because of their position, these men hold great influence over the minds of the populace. And the world these churchmen describe as real is, above all, spiritual. They are creating a reality which places their idea about God's plan for mankind at the very center of life. . . .

"Life is about passing a spiritual test, you discover. The churchmen explain that God has placed mankind at the center of his universe, surrounded by the entire cosmos, for one solitary purpose: to win or lose salvation. And in this trial you must correctly choose between two opposing forces: the force of God and the lurking temptations of the devil.

"But understand that you don't face this contest alone," he continued. "In fact, as a mere individual you aren't qualified to determine your status in this regard. This is the province of the churchmen; they are there to interpret the scriptures and to tell you every step of the way whether you are in accordance with God or whether you are being duped by Satan. If you follow their instructions, you are assured that a rewarding afterlife will follow. But if you fail to heed the course they prescribe, then, well . . . there is excommunication and certain damnation." [1]

This power of the church to control entry into the afterlife is pure fiction. But the domination is real (in the human sense).

Church leaders in my childhood faith claimed to emulate Jesus the Christ. Yet their outward appearance belied that intent. Jesus has traditionally been portrayed as an educated but poor man. A man whose daily life revolved around service to the ill, the poor, and the disenfranchised. The classic portrait of Jesus washing the feet of a woman tells it all. He was a religious man who humbled himself in order to glorify Yahweh.

My childhood impression was that a Catholic priest's role bespoke more royal governance than humble service. Priests in my childhood parishes wore brightly colored silk vestments and paraded into church following a court of altar boys, some carrying gold and incense. On special occasions, the priest would even be carried into church on a golden chair raised high above the shoulders of the parishioners drafted to carry it. To me, these grand entrances reflect more of a medieval kingdom than God's kingdom. I did notice that no one else seemed offended by this radical departure from the example Christ set, presumably because human animal tradition demands that the alpha male be exulted and others bow, literally or figuratively. Humans are used to hierarchy in religion as in life.

Notwithstanding some very dark ages, people of all callings and stations have for over two thousand years kept alive a tradition and way of thinking and living called Christianity. Most equate the religion with fellowship and brotherly love, a decidedly spiritual leaning. Most believe in one God, another universal truth. And most long fervently to be reunited with their Creator in everlasting bliss—a belief that springs from the everlasting truth of our eternal oneness with Source. The kernels of Universal Knowledge are there in Christianity. And no amount of human animal fear or survival instinct can extinguish these truths in the hearts of those who walk their spiritual paths as best they know how.

> *I understand from just reliving human history that, overall, no individual is more important than another to Source. No one. No significance is attributed to the life of Abraham, Jesus, Muhammad, or any other religious figure. Millions of people throughout history are briefly presented as prophets and truth-givers—men and women whose enlightenment shines through for the education and inspiration of others. But they are ordinary people who did not start religions.*

> *No Savior, Messiah, Christ or Son of God is identified anywhere on the planet in the millions of*

years of Earth chronicles unfolding before me. And that is completely consistent with what I absorbed earlier in the afterlife from Universal Knowledge about the truth of our existence. Yet I am rocked to the very core of my being by this revelation.

Watching this panorama of human religious history, I feel much like a parent who watches a child learning to walk—loving all her attempts, failures, and successes equally, though knowing she has a long way to go yet, and loving that too. While I watch, the part of me that had played the role of the human named Nanci rails against the injustice done by religions. Yet, in my renewed natural state as a Light Being, I find it all wonderfully quaint, charming, and intellectually fascinating. My attitude toward mankind's evolution reflects the same unconditional love my Light Being friends felt for me earlier in this experience while reviewing my human life. I do not judge.

Throughout the documentary, knowings informed me that religion has tremendous capacity to comfort and inspire us. But, as with everything else in life, we are not all comforted and uplifted by the same words, thoughts, or beliefs. A belief, such as salvation can only be gained through Jesus, that launches one heart into the stratosphere of religious ecstasy may strike another as condescending, or worse, accusatory. We each hold dear different truths about life, death, and the afterlife. Our lives are unique and our diverse experiences craft our beliefs like individual snowflakes.

Those who are relatively like-minded in their beliefs may find companionship and support in religions organized around them. Such groups have contributed millions of hours and dollars to the betterment of their fellow humans. These groups do a disservice to mankind, however, when they ensconce themselves in the human herd mentality. One religion is not better than another; one belief system may not be perfectly suited for all. Those Light Being souls who have incarnated in humans for only a few lifetimes will find more comfort in the more primitive human belief systems, just as early man did. Light Being souls who have been here many times and carry some memory of who they truly are, on the other hand, may gravitate to spiritual philosophies that resonate with their innate knowledge of Source. Any belief system, or none at all, is fine with Source for nothing can change the fact that we exist entirely within Source and therefore cannot be deprived of that heavenly union.

15

Earth's Future and End

THE HISTORY OF RELIGION THAT I witnessed in the afterlife documentary was nestled within a panoramic view of Earth's lifespan—including its end. I watched Earth's future without much interest because I was convinced I would not be returning to human life. It was my time to die. Consequently, I made no effort to remember future events until I realized that my soul would again imminently commingle with my former human body.

I remember a few dramatic scenes from the future (that is, post-1994, the year I died). They are:

> *Habitation on Earth occurs in three cycles of thousands to millions of years each, identified as epochs. ("Epoch" is one of only about a dozen English words used during my time in the afterlife so I attach significance to it.) Epochs are bookended by major planetary changes. Earth is currently very near the end of its Second Epoch. The major transitional events ushering in the Third Epoch begin in what I estimate to be 2013-14. I cannot be certain of the timeframe because nothing I see is dated. My distinct impression, however, is that the Third Epoch begins sometime during what would have been Nanci's remaining lifetime (1950 -?).*
>
> *Unlike the change from First to Second Epochs, which involved continental drift and Earth orbit changes, the*

transition to the Third Epoch does not spell Armageddon for the planet itself. I detect some changes in Earth's tilt and rotation but nothing that would preclude human habitation. The planetary changes are not significant enough to attract most humans' attention.

Hundreds to thousands of natural disasters, which increase in frequency and intensity as the Second Epoch comes to a close, pockmark the transition between epochs. I witness earthquakes, tsunamis, flooding along coastlines and rivers, extreme weather and climate changes, monster storms, and volcanic eruptions.

Non-lethal bacteria and viruses mutate into antibiotic-resistant diseases and sweep Earth in pandemics, decimating the population. (Today's outbreaks of SARS, MERSA, *E. coli*, and CRPK fulfill this prophecy.) *Other, previously survivable illnesses also become deadly.*

The combination of natural disasters and pandemics ultimately reduces the human race to roughly one-quarter or less of its pre-Third Epoch numbers. Knowings inform me that each person who dies during the transition does so voluntarily at a time of his/her own choosing. Each Light Being soul is given the option of staying on Earth or going home to what we call the afterlife. The decision turns on whether the soul believes it can best effect a smoother epoch transition by remaining in human life or returning to spiritual form.

There are no global or nuclear wars in the future. Instead, I see death and destruction rain down as the result of human misbehavior, especially our failure to maintain proper stewardship of the planet.

As I pull back for an aerial view of Earth, the number of objects of all sizes and descriptions orbiting our sun astounds me. The typical solar system model used in American education is profoundly misleading. I watch American astronomers discover what I term "gas giants" throughout our galaxy. These celestial bodies are vividly colorful swirling masses of gases and debris in roughly circular shape. (The discovery of these gaseous masses was reported in the newspapers on May 21, 2011, in articles exclaiming that scientists have discovered a quintupling of the previously estimated number of gas giants in the universe.)

Perched just outside our solar system I have a view of a tenth planet beyond Jupiter, orbiting our sun. It appears to be composed mostly of rock and ice, but it is not a comet. I am crazy with excitement to be the first human to know that our solar system has more planets than scientists ever imagined. (Astronomers discovered this planet on November 14, 2003, and named it Sedna. This discovery, among others, prompted the scientific community to question the planet classification system. They concluded that our complement of "planets" consists of the four gas giants named Jupiter, Neptune, Saturn and Uranus, the two orbiting ice balls named Pluto and Sedna, and four terrestrial planets named Earth, Mars, Mercury and Venus.)

Zooming in to the height of a satellite orbiting Earth, I notice that Japan is gone. The entire island has vanished. I cannot discern the cause. (Thus the news reports in March 2011 caused me grave concern: Japan had moved eighteen feet east and had sunk two to four feet as the result of an 8.9 offshore earthquake.)

Similarly, I note that portions of the United States' familiar topography are different. Parts of the East Coast are missing or flooded, including New York City and bedroom communities up and down the East Coast, which have dropped below sea level. Florida's southern peninsula is gone leaving only the landmass attached to Georgia and Alabama. The Mississippi River basin is so flooded that Louisiana is nearly completely under water, along with half of each state to the north to about Kentucky. (Natural flooding and Army Corps of Engineers' release of dams in 2011 may be precursors.) *The entire West Coast has vanished from just south of Big Sur to the Baja Peninsula. Mountains form the new California coastline, which plunges precipitously to the Pacific. (I do not recall the name of the mountain range.)*

The final event I see in the Second-to-Third epoch transition period is the collapse of the world's financial systems, which forces human reorganization into smaller, more agrarian societies. The United States' government bails out insurance companies that become insolvent after paying out huge amounts of their reserves in natural disaster claims. Next the government bails out utilities. The federal government eventually goes bankrupt from the fiscal strain of the bailouts. (Naturally, I panicked when the AIG bailout was reported in the news in

2008.)

The Third Epoch is much shorter but calmer and more peaceful than the preceding two eras. The human population is greatly reduced inasmuch as only those able to overcome human violent tendencies survive the transition to participate in this tranquil period.

Knowings explain that the universe is currently in the "back swing" of Creation's parabolic curve. The universe is an oval-shaped Energy explosion out of Source that is shrinking, returning to end where it began—in Source. Everything in the universe is now in the return phase of the journey.

As the end of the documentary approaches, I watch my beloved planet become uninhabitable and say to myself: "Oh, it goes just like Mars did." Earth and Mars now resemble fraternal twins—red, dry, desolate and devoid of life. The human species is gone. Extinct.

My final thought before the curtain closes is: "It was a wild ride."

A few other afterlife experiencers were likewise gifted with visions of Earth's future. The most famous are Dannion Brinkley's, described in his first book, *Saved by the Light.*[1] Dannion pens a vivid visual collage: television-like boxes of scenes of future earth events zooming at him from the chests of Beings of Light. He actually experienced all the events that were projected at him as though he was there. After returning to his body, Dannion wrote down 117 of the future events he remembered. Between 1978 and 1994, ninety-five of the predictions came true, including Ronald Reagan becoming president and the Chernobyl nuclear power plant disaster.[2]

Similarly, while he was in the afterlife, near-death experiencer Ned Dougherty foresaw that "a major terrorist attack may befall New York City or Washington, D.C., severely impacting the way we live in the United States."[3] This certainly sounds like the 9/11 terrorist attacks. Ned Dougherty, a happy drug and alcohol abuser, died in 1984 at age thirty-seven of a heart attack after trying to strangle a business associate to death. Ned was a Catholic college graduate, a successful real estate agent, and owner of the most exclusive private nightclub in the Hamptons at the time of his NDE.

Dannion and Ned independently reported viewing an Earth future replete with all manner of natural disasters. Ned witnessed the following upcoming events during his time in the Light:

I watched as the axis of Earth's rotation began to shift significantly. . . . Great earthquakes erupted throughout the world, significantly changing the major continents. There were volcanic eruptions of great magnitude spewing clouds of billowing smoke and ash throughout the atmosphere, sending the Earth into a period of darkness. Great floods resulted from melting and shifting polar ice caps. Many low-lying land areas were engulfed by huge tidal waves.[4]

Ned's description more closely resembles what I saw in the transition period between the First and Second Earth Epochs than any future events. But time does not exist in the afterlife, making it very difficult to pinpoint past and future. NDE researcher and psychologist Kenneth Ring relates a colleague's comment that he had interviewed several near-death experiencers who had witnessed Earth's future. All of them reported essentially the same story: widespread and cataclysmic destruction—to occur in 1988![5] While writing *Heading Toward Omega*, Dr. Ring interviewed sixteen additional NDErs who concur with the dire predictions of the then future 1980s:

> There is, first of all, a sense of having total knowledge,
> but specifically one is aware of seeing the entirety of the
> earth's evolution and history, from the beginning to the end
> of time. The future scenario, however, is usually of short
> duration, seldom extending much beyond the beginning of
> the twenty-first century. The individuals report that in this
> decade there will be an increasing incidence of earthquakes,
> volcanic activity, and generally massive geophysical changes.
> There will be resultant disturbances in weather patterns and
> food supplies. The world economic system will collapse,
> and the possibility of nuclear war or accident is very great
> (respondents are not agreed on *whether* a nuclear catastrophe
> will occur). All of these events are transitional rather than
> ultimate, however, and they will be followed by a new era
> in human history marked by human brotherhood, universal
> love, and world peace. Though many will die, the earth will
> live. While agreeing that the dates for these events are not
> fixed, most individuals feel that they are likely to take place
> during the 1980s.[6]

Apparently the dates of the shift in epochs are not cast in stone, judging from what actually happened in the 1980s. Or perhaps the transition has been postponed—and may be again.

Modern-day prophets who have dared make their knowledge of the future public, like Ken Ring's NDErs, have proven inaccurate often enough that the public largely ignores them. Global communication technology allows us to instantaneously witness most major events. So it is easy to determine and widely broadcast the *perceived* accuracy of a prophecy after the fact. But is this sufficient reason to reject the messages of love and hope afterlife experiencers offer us alongside their mistaken prophecies?

Often a future prediction is wrong due only to a misunderstanding of the events foreseen. The popular television show *Medium*, starring Patricia Arquette and Jake Weber, explored the various misinterpretations of visions by real-life psychic Allison DuBois, whose career includes helping law enforcement officers investigate crimes. For example, in one episode Allison dreamed that a candidate running against her boss for District Attorney was standing behind her boss's desk, using his telephone, surrounded by boxes of packed office furnishings. She logically assumed her boss was going to lose the up-coming election. At the end of the show, however, viewers see Allison's vision revealed as totally benign. The opposing candidate explains to the bewildered DA that he (the candidate) had lost his keys and used the DA's office to call his wife to pick him up. The DA's belongings were packed in boxes because his office was to be fumigated the next day. Allison's vision was totally accurate. However, her interpretation of it missed the mark.

In the same way, I misinterpreted some visions I had of the future during my beyond death experience in 1994. I remember seeing an aerial view of India with the mouth of the River Ganges darkened, as if it had been flooded or sank out of sight. My assumption upon resuming human life was that the land mass was destroyed. But I was wrong. I saw this exact aerial view in the newspaper on January 26, 2001. It was a satellite photo of 32 million Hindus crowding the confluence of the Ganges and Yamura Rivers for the Millennium celebration of the Kumbh festival. The presence of so many people darkened the earth in the view from space, making it appear as though the land had submerged. My beleif that water rather than people had flooded the landmass was reasonable in light of the many other instances of flooding I witnessed.

Whatever else the many prophetic visions NDErs have in the afterlife may or may not tell us, they do dispel the accuracy of the 3-D movie-worthy scenes of the book of Revelation. All of NDErs' visions of the future reflect typically earthly phenomena.

The book of Revelation, of course, is the most publicized Christian prediction of mankind's alleged future. The manuscript was included in the New Testament as an example of a well-known Jewish apocalyptic literary genre of the late first or early second century, not because of its prophetic credibility. Several other apocalyptic writings are included in the Old Testament as well as the Nag Hammadi Library of third and fourth-century Coptic manuscripts.[7] Apocalyptic writings surfaced in the Judeo-Christian tradition whenever the Jews were persecuted for their religion. At the time the book of Revelation was written, the Roman emperor Nero is reputed to have slaughtered Jewish and gentile Christians for refusing to worship Nero as a god. The book of Revelation, therefore, was intended more as a political oratory than an account of actual future predictions.

The most important knowing I received about Earth's future came long before the historical documentary played out in my mind. Earlier in my afterlife experience I had learned volumes about a phenomenon labeled with one of the few other English words to reach my spiritual ears: *manifesting*. The knowings clarified that all of those Light Being characters within Source who have an interest in mankind collectively manifest what humans experience as physical reality. Unfortunately, those who have chosen to inhabit human animals as their souls have allowed human nature to affect their manifesting. Thus Earth itself now reflects the human character traits of violence, waste, and self-destruction. But circumstances can change, and change dramatically, if enough of us souls awaken to our true nature and take conscious control over how we create and maintain the Earth manifestation.

16

Religion Is for Humans

THE AFTERLIFE DOCUMENTARY TAUGHT ME that religion is for humans—and for us Light Beings too while we share humans' lives. Religion is our way of reconciling the eternal truths we know in our spiritual hearts with the pain and violence we experience in human lives that seem so *real,* but are so foreign to our nature as Source. The amnesia of entering into the human manifestation blinds us to our true nature, resulting in belief systems that arise from human character traits, fear, and superstitions.

Religious beliefs cradle the images and dreams we have of an afterlife and immortality. These beliefs comfort us upon the loss of a loved one and sustain us through hardship and strife. Organized religions focus our faith, hope, and beliefs as a community to help us reach the goal of eternal life. Religions' ranks of believers nurture our children, support our marriages, and nurse us back to health or acceptance of death when our time has come to leave this mortal realm. Tremendous good has been done in the name of religions, including providing disaster relief, feeding the poor, offering prayers for the downhearted, and establishing world-famous institutions of higher learning and hospitals.

Religion has served a valuable role in civilization. In order for humans to live peaceably in societies, rules and laws must be adopted and enforced among its members. It is a scientific fact that humans are animals. And as such, their behavior must be controlled lest they revert to wilderness ways. Traditionally, religions adopt and follow various codes of behavior, which are then imposed on the entire membership. The code may be as minimal as the Ten Commandments, or as sophisticated as the Qur'an, the Bible, or Hindu scriptures. But the moral codes religions offer us generally keep us safe.

Although bits of eternal truth are woven into various belief systems, religions are essentially manmade and therefore rife with human error. Humans cannot rise above their innate nature. They have no choice to disregard their fears and hopes. They cannot be anything other than what Source designed them to be—animals leading animal lives on a wild, lush, fascinating planet.

But we are not humans. Though we inhabit their bodies, we are not constrained by human nature or traits. We remain the powerful, eternal, resourceful characters/parts of Source no matter where we seem to be in the physical world. We *can* rise above animal nature and embrace the eternal truths of our birthright, even here on Earth. There is no divine mandate that we do so. In fact, Source designed its consciousness characters precisely to experience what being wholly human is like. And to experience the lives and character traits of all creatures throughout the universe as well.

Yet Source-self-awareness cannot be denied forever. Eventually, after numerous incarnations, we begin to remember bits and pieces of eternal truths. Our memories arise in the form of intuition, inspiration, or a distinct internal resonance with something we hear or read. For those of us whose enlightenment allows us to remember who we really are, religion may no longer hold the attraction it once did. Those who remember are here to serve those who do not, to help them awaken to their own innate ability to rediscover the truth—not to assume roles as dictators of truth.

Readers sometimes ask me why our current religions have

survived the test of time if they are manmade. My answer: they have thrived *because* they are manmade. Because they so accurately portray *human* nature, not Source's nature, religions speak directly to the human heart. Religious institutions have been designed to play to well-understood aspects of human nature.

For example, humans are herd animals. There are natural leaders in any group and the rest are followers. There is absolutely nothing shameful about being a follower. It is nature's design for this species. Source built the herd mentality right into our hosts' innate character traits. Organized religions unconsciously rely upon this known fact. They create herds of believers for their particular brand of dogma and elevate the natural leaders among their members to positions of church leadership. The leaders are called priests, ministers, lamas, gurus, and other appellations of respect and recognition, conferring status based on a calling, superior knowledge of God's will, education level, or even prophet status.

Everyone else in an organized religion becomes a follower. The flock (not a coincidental word choice by religion) feels secure with its chosen leadership. Members of the congregation adopt what the leader proclaims to be the truth. Individual interpretation of scripture is discouraged. Some organized religions expressly prohibit their followers from reading sacred scripture and forming their own conclusions. The Roman Catholic Church even goes so far as to state that only its Pope can infallibly determine God's truth. In my youth, Catholics were discouraged from self-reflection and required to rely upon the clergy for our sole access to the truths of the afterlife.

The herd of faithful does not question authority. Nor do they care much about thinking deeply about what members are learning. It seems quite natural to us, and is entirely consistent with human animal nature, to be passive vessels accepting dogma being poured into us by our religions' leaders. Religious organizations depend upon this acceptance for their survival.

Individual spirituality goes against the grain of human nature. Not only that, it actually threatens the stability of the herd. Opportunities for power or control by one human over others vanish when each of us individually seeks guidance from within, from our own connection to Universal Knowledge. There is no way to amass an enormous flock of followers if each of us seeks out and embraces our own individual truths. Speaking more basely, there is no way to make money from a spirituality that does not depend upon paying others for guidance, interpretation of scripture, healing, or assurance about salvation. So those who have profited from religion, and those who are securely entrenched in their follower status, rebel against a spiritual model in which everyone discovers his/her own answers to the great questions of life. They fight it with every tool they can imagine, including calling anything that threatens their thinking "the work of the Devil."

Those who consider themselves gatekeepers of the truth—the humans whose jobs grant them the right to interpret religious writings and dogma—fight self-directed spirituality the most. A society that promotes self-discovery strips these gatekeepers of their power. And humans with the innate leadership character trait are vehement about their right to hold power over others. Some convince themselves that their right to control the flow of religious truths is God-given. They refer to it as a "calling" from God, even though they are the ones who sought religion as a career path and chose to stick with it through the rigors of modern religious leadership training.

Surprisingly, some of us fight just as strenuously to maintain our right to be followers of a chosen religious spokesman. We actually argue for the right not to think, do, question, or otherwise actively participate in our own spiritual development. We are not only content to be spoon-fed someone else's beliefs, we insist upon it. That way we can fulfill our own concept of faith by merely being physically present at a religious service or observance. We do not have to work for our answers. Humans prefer not to work when they can avoid it. So, our current structure of organized religions fits perfectly with the attitude of the great majority of humankind.

In the final analysis, religion is primarily for and about humans, not the Light Being souls within them. No one religion or belief system can guarantee humans the afterlife that we Light Being souls will experience automatically as part of our spiritual nature. As two near-death experiencers so eloquently explain:

> "God couldn't care less about religion," exclaimed one woman. An Australian near-death experiencer added, "They say that if you're not a Christian none of you will be able to come in through the eye of the needle, and all that sort of thing. And I think, well, I went up there and I saw it and I certainly wasn't a Christian at the time."[1]

My sojourn in the afterlife, and especially the experience of watching the documentary of man's religious developments, revealed a wealth of eternal truths beyond those available through human belief systems. Revered academic scholars who have come to these truths the hard way—through rigorous study of human writings, artifacts, and history—have offered some of these concepts to the masses, readily available in books written for laymen. Near-death experiencers have likewise braved criticism and ridicule to share intensely personal accounts of their brushes with eternity.

My vision of religious history convinced me that we have been listening to the wrong message—a human animal religious message.

It is time to stop listening. Fear of change is uniquely human. I *knew* that as fact while transitioning back to human life from the afterlife. Yet my host body Nanci still *felt* the fear. And I experienced it along with her. It still influenced my thinking despite my knowledge to the contrary. Many months went by before I was able to shake the fear of changes that I knew lay ahead of me after my return to human life. How much stronger the fear must be for those who have not had the benefit of an afterlife experience like mine to reassure them that Source exists regardless of our fears to the contrary. It is perfectly understandable that churchmen and churchwomen who have not accessed Universal Knowledge would cling to writings represented to them for millennia to be messages from Source. Yet, one should study the origin of such writings before committing to believe them.

17

Our Place in the Universe

RELIVING MANKIND'S CREATION AND WATCH-ING humans evolve in my afterlife documentary convinced me that many of our most deeply held beliefs are delusions. Humans are not the center of the universe. The millions of other planets and galaxies are not uninhabited. Our earthly lives are not the end-all and be-all of creation. We are not the most important creatures in the universe—yet we are far more important than we believe.

Humans are animals. Nothing more. And nothing less. They serve as host bodies for us—Source's consciousness characters inhabiting them as Light Being souls. Humans are part of the manifested physical world Source created in order to experience events and emotions unavailable in a purely spiritual state. We are not human. So we need not be limited to their self-centered animal view of creation.

Humans are self-absorbed by nature. A creature whose only goal in life is physical survival is by design limited in perspective. Psychologists may call completely self-focused people narcissistic, or some other name from the big book of personality disorders, implying they are abnormal. But they are not. Humans are innately selfish because that trait promotes survival. Each of us is self-involved from time to time, and to greater or lesser degrees, all the time. We spiritual beings inside humans experience self-centeredness when we allow our hosts' innate nature to dominate our lives.

Humans have been self-absorbed in their perception of the

universe. Mankind's view of the structure of the world stems from its observation of the hierarchical structure of the plant and animal kingdoms. It is therefore logical and reasonable for humans to assume that hierarchies exist elsewhere within the universe, and between Source and man. Such a rudimentary animal viewpoint is far too limited, however, to serve us well as spiritual beings.

Just as the timing was right when Galileo Galilee was excommunicated by the Catholic Church[1] for pronouncing that the Earth rotated around the sun, which conflicted with man's belief that humans are the center of creation, it is time for us now to adopt a more enlightened view of mankind's place in the universe though it may conflict with our religions.

There is no hierarchy in the universe from Source's perspective. We are all one with Source. We are all part of the same eternal, all-powerful, all-knowing, all-loving Creative Energy. Every single molecule is equal to every other molecule. Every rock, bird, tree, and human is equal to the other. From Source's perspective, the only difference between a human body and a rock is the Energy signature or density level of its physical matter. Both may be invested with Source self-awareness. If you raise a rock's Energy level high enough, it might likewise exhibit recognizable characteristics of a Light Being soul. It will be sentient and self-aware because of its nature as part of Source. It is time for us to know that humans are an equally important part of the totality of creation, though no more important than any other part.

It is also time to acknowledge our true power as Beings of Light because our adopted-from-humans self-centered, animalistic view of our place in the grand scheme has obscured that power. We are not part of God in the way we have always understood. We are far more. When Christians say they are part of the Body of Christ, the meaning is allegorical. No one really believes himself/herself to be a skin cell or toe, for example, on an enormous physical body. When someone says he is "part" of a family, he means genetically. And even though families share the same DNA, family members consider themselves completely separate individuals. Sometimes when a woman says she is part of someone else, she means emotionally, but she still acknowledges that though an emotional tie exists, it is between two separate beings. Or people may mean they have a history of shared experiences with other individuals when they say they are part of each other. Similarly, when religions say "we are part of God," it is meant metaphorically.

When I tell you we are part of Source, however, I mean it in the literal sense. We are part of Source in the same way your arms and legs are part of your human body. It is an unembellished meaning. There is no separation into individuals. Our eternal constituency within Source is far more than sharing DNA, an emotional attachment, or shared history of experiences. It is an absolute factual sameness. And we must recognize our power and our place in the universe because of that fact.

Once we understand that everything is connected, is part of one continuous whole, and that the whole is the God humans have been worshiping for thousands of years, our perspective will naturally change. We will see that everything that surrounds us is just as deserving of our love, honor, and respect as Source is. Every single part of the universe is just as alive as we are, and is just as much a part of Source as we are. And we need to start treating our planet and one another with the same love, honor, respect, and worship that traditionally has been reserved for God.

Pollution, deforestation, hunting species to extinction, and ignoring Mother Earth's warning signs that the environment is in danger cannot be justified by the desire for creature comforts. The deterioration in our habitat cannot reach crisis proportions, a doomsday scenario, before we notice it. Still today humans merely treat the symptoms, providing relief to tsunami victims, for example, while turning a blind eye to the increasingly urgent pleas of our planet for attention to its health. Human shortsightedness is destroying this planet.

Discrimination between species of animals, and among humans themselves on the basis of skin color, gender, handicap, or sexual preference cannot be justified. All physical matter is composed of the same eternal Energy. How can a person honestly claim that the electricity in his toaster is better than the electricity in his garage door opener? Energy is Energy. The pattern it takes adds nothing to its intrinsic value. We are all Source Energy regardless of form, and that Energy is uniform by nature.

We must wake up to the fact that though human animals are the kings of a material hierarchy, we are not humans! We are so much more important than that, because we have an intimate connection to all of Creation. Everything we do affects every other part of the whole. Just as stretching one part of a rubber band, or pushing your thumb into a ball of Play-Doh, changes its structure, our actions change the nature of everything around us. Our planet is suffering the effects of our belief that we are separate from it. If you doubt that, read the Millennium Ecosystem Assessment Report published March 30, 2005, by a global team of 1,300 scientists. Our interpersonal relationships are suffering the effects of our belief that we are separate from each other, and from Source. If you doubt that, watch any TV newscast.

The time has come for us to begin again with a fresh perspective. It is time to break out of our cocoons of amnesia and emerge resplendent in the awareness and love of our Light Being selves. We are more than human animals doomed to death and decomposition. We are living aspects of Source awareness capable of creating reality in concert with all of the universe, our equal partners in the manifesting process, as we trip from experience to experience sampling Source's imagination and love in all its many forms.

Appendix

A Few NDE Facts and Opinions

RAYMOND MOODY, MD, COINED THE TERM "near-death experience" (NDE) in his landmark first book on the subject, *Life After Life*, (New York: Bantum Books 1975).

Although "near-death" may be descriptive of the phenomenon for scientific purposes, those who have gone through it would say there is nothing "near" about it. We were truly dead—in my case from anaphylactic shock during an invasive radiological procedure. NDErs experience life after death with an even greater degree of reality than we each experienced, for instance, grade school, our first kiss, and lunch today. Life outside the body is not simply a dream or hallucination to us, any more than you would consider experiencing your marriage, or the work you do today, to be a *dream* rather than fact.

Cardiologist and researcher Pim von Lommel, MD, of the Netherlands, related in his 2006 presentation at the International Association for Near-Death Studies Conference at MD Anderson Medical Center that perhaps ten million Americans have died and returned to human life. According to Dr. von Lommel's review of the research, between 24% and 40% of individuals who come close to death report one or more aspects of a near-death experience. His paper, "Pleasurable Western Adult NDEs," is available from the International Association for Near-Death Studies at www.iands.org.

The three most well-known autobiographical NDE books are *90 Minutes in Heaven* by Don Piper with Cecil Murphey (New York: Revell 2004), a moving story of Rev. Piper's recovery from mortal injuries sustained in an automobile accident that includes a brief NDE featuring going into the Light and meeting deceased loved ones, but stops short of entering what the author describes as heaven; Betty J. Eadie's *Embraced by The Light* (Carson City, NV: Gold Leaf Press 1992), the inspirational account of a transcendental afterlife experience describing entering into the Light, meeting Beings of Light, receiving Universal Knowledge, and having a life review; and Dannion Brinkley with Paul Perry, *Saved by the Light: The True Story of A Man Who Died Twice and the Profound Revelations He Received* (New York: Harper Paperbacks 1994), a wealth of revelations about the afterlife in one of the most extensive and detailed accounts published. Mr. Brinkley's death after being struck by lightening while talking on the telephone resulted in his entering into the Light, meeting Beings of Light, visiting a crystal City of Light, receiving Universal Knowledge, having a life review, and witnessing visions of Earth's future.

NDE accounts are an excellent source of information, in my opinion, because their authors are eyewitnesses to eternal life. To a lawyer, like me, eyewitness testimony is the most credible form of testimony. I am aware that scientific studies have shown that eyewitness perceptions can be decidedly wrong, due to errors in human sensory perception and the psychology of bearing witness to dramatic events. But, I believe that being out of body cures all human sensory perception errors because the experiencer is no longer limited to the body's senses. That, to me, gives the NDE narrative more credibility than any other type of eyewitness account.

The NDEr may well still be limited to human mental perspective, however, if his/her afterlife experience does not progress to the stage when human perspective is washed away and replaced with the spiritual understanding of our natural state. An experiencer's ability to comprehend knowings from Universal Knowledge changes dramatically the deeper into the Light he/she goes. For example, someone who enters into the Light and progresses no farther into the afterlife may mistake the Light itself to be Source. He may think he has merged into Source. Someone who progresses through the entire afterlife transition and merges into Source, on the other hand, will be able to look backwards and see that the Light is just the beginning of Source's "aura" (for lack of a better term).

As we progress through the afterlife transition, and raise our awareness and understanding to more sophisticated levels, different "truths" resonate with us. What feels right at one level of enlightenment or experience might be deemed slightly misunderstood or off the mark at another level. For this reason, I believe near-death and afterlife accounts should be read in light of how far into the transition process the experiencer progressed. In other words, was the experience deep enough that the experiencer escaped human perspective and was able to relate "knowings" from the spiritual level of understanding?

Knowing whether an NDEr made the shift in perspective from human to spiritual is important because all knowledge absorbed at any level in the afterlife is absolutely convincing—far more compelling than anything experienced in human life. An experiencer who barely enters the afterlife will be completely convinced of his/ her interpretation of events without realizing the interpretation comes from human beliefs. When that same NDEr progresses deeper into the afterlife, he might well completely change the interpretation he found so convincing earlier in the experience just by virtue of the shift from human perspective to spiritual. For example, someone who goes into the Light and sees beautiful gardens, but goes no further, may well be absolutely certain that heaven consists of an earth-like physical paradise. If that same soul had gone deeper into the afterlife, however, the NDEr might well have learned that the gardens are manifestations (illusions) and that there exist no physical matter environments in a purely spiritual afterlife.

Finally, as with everything else we read, we must consider the NDE account author's educational, experiential, and religious backgrounds as those will be the sources from which the author will draw his/her language choices to describe what essentially cannot be related in words. For example, someone with a PhD in physics may interpret something differently than another person with an eighth grade education. A world traveler will have experiences from which to draw analogies that are unknown to an NDEr who has never traveled outside his/her home state. And, an experiencer with early childhood religious training will fall back on those concepts to explain the afterlife.

Many articles on near-death experiences and afterlife accounts are available on the websites sponsored by the International Association for Near-Death Studies, www.iands.org; the Near-Death Research Foundation, at www.nderf.org; and at researcher/author Kevin Williams' website of www.near-death.com. Video clips of NDE and afterlife accounts appear on YouTube.

NOTES

Chapter 1

[1]   Kenneth Ring, *Lessons From the Light: What We Can Learn From the Near-Death Experience* (Needham, MA: Moment Point Press, 1998), 295-296.

[2]   Ibid., 298.

[3]   Betty J. Eadie, *Embraced by the Light* (Carson City, NV: Gold Leaf Press, 1992), 43-44.

[4]   Richard Elliott Friedman, *Who Wrote the Bible?* (New York: HarperCollins, 1987). Dr. Friedman is the Ann and Jay Davis Professor of Jewish Studies at the University of Georgia, and held the Katzin Chair at the University of California at San Diego when this, his most popular work, was published. Dr. Friedman works in eight languages, including ancient Akkadian, Aramaic, Greek and Hebrew.

[5]   Ibid., 16, 30-31.

[6]   Ibid., 87.

[7]   Stephen L. Harris, *Understanding the Bible: A Reader's Introduction*, (New York: Mayfield Publishing, 1985). *Also see,* Burton L. Mack, *Who Wrote the New Testament? The Making of the Christian Myth,* (New York: HarperCollins, 1995). Now retired, Dr. Mack was a Professor of Early Christianity at the Claremont School of Theology at Claremont and Associate Scholar at the Institute of Antiquity and Christianity in Clermont at the time.

[8]   Bart D. Ehrman, *Misquoting Jesus: The Story Behind Who Changed the Bible and Why* (New York: HarperCollins, 2005).

[9]   Ibid., 11-12.

Chapter 2

[1]   Eadie, *Embraced by the Light,* 46-48.

[2]   Ring, *Lessons From the Light,* 288.

[3]   Genesis 1:6 – 1:26.

[4]   Genesis 2:4 – 2:24.

[5]   Friedman, *Who Wrote the Bible,* 50-51.

[6]   The Holy Qur'an, 7:54. All references to the Qur'an are to the University of Virginia translation and online edition (2009).

[7]   P.M.H. Atwater, *Future Memory* (Charlottesville, VA: Hampton Roads, 1999), 152.

[8]   See Chapter 17 of my first book, *BACKWARDS: Returning to Our Source for Answers,* and Chapter 12 of my second book, *BACKWARDS Guidebook,* for a discussion on manifesting physical reality.

[9]   Genesis 1:1 –1:31.

Chapter 3

[1]   I use the term "characters" here in the same sense as I used the word "Sourcebeams" and "Beings of Light" in my first book, *BACKWARDS: Returning to Our Source for Answers.* I have struggled to find an accurate-enough phrase or word to describe this completely non-human concept for which no English word has been created. So, I have used "aspects," "parts," "fragments" and "subdivision" of Source, as well as "personalities" within Source.

[2]   Heaven and the afterlife are described in detail in Chapter 6 of *BACKWARDS: Returning to Our Source for Answers.*

[3]   Leonard ___, "Leonard NDE 4046," author's summary of near-death experience, Near-Death Experience Research Foundation website, www.nderf.org.

[4]   David Goines, "David Goines' NDE," author's summary of near-death experience, Kevin Williams, Webmaster, Near-Death Experiences and the Afterlife, www.near-death.com/children.html.

Chapter 4

[1]   George G. Ritchie with Elizabeth Sherrill, *Return from Tomorrow* (Grand Rapids, MI: Fleming H. Revell, 1978), 61-62.

[2]   Ibid., 64-65.

[3]   Ibid., 67.

[4]   Dannion Brinkley with Paul Perry, *Saved by the Light: The True Story of A Man Who Died Twice and the Profound Revelations He Received* (New York: HarperCollins, 1994). A made-for-TV movie based on the book was aired in December 1995. Watching the movie, I realized for the first time in physical life that I had died on March 14, 1994 and had gone into the afterlife.

[5]   Dannion Brinkley with Kathryn Brinkley, *Secrets of the Light: Lessons from Heaven* (New York: HarperCollins, 2008), 78.

[6]   Ibid., 78-79.

[7]   Ibid., 82.

[8]   Ibid., 83, 84.

[9]   T. J. Wray and Gregory Mobley, *The Birth of Satan: Tracing the Devil's Biblical Roots* (New York: Palgrave Macmillan, 2005), 5. Dr. Tina Wray is Assistant Professor of Religious Studies at Salve Regina University, Newport, RI. Gregory Mobley, PhD, is Associate Professor of Old Testament at Andover Newton Theological School and an ordained American Baptist Minister.

[10]   Ibid., 39. The spelling of Yahweh without vowels more accurately reflects the original language, according to Professors Wray and Mobley.

[11]   Robert Wright, *The Evolution of God* (New York: Little, Brown, 2009), 166.

[12]   Jeffrey Burton Russell, *The Devil: Perceptions of Evil from Antiquity to Primitive Christianity* (Ithaca, NY: Cornell University Press, 1977), 176-77.

[13]   Wray and Mobley cite a specific example where King David is said in 2 Samuel 24 to have been incited by the Lord's anger to count the people. The parallel account written centuries later in 1 Chronicles 21 says that Satan incited David to count the people. Wray and Mobley, *Birth of Satan,* 44.

14 Wray and Mobley, *Birth of Satan,* 70.

15 Ibid., 70-71, 86-87, 149-153.

16 Ibid., 151, quoting Paul Carus, *The History of the Devil and the Idea of Evil* (New York: Gramercy Books, 1996).

Chapter 5

1 Genesis 2:7.

2 Ibid.

3 *The Holy Qur'an, al-Hijr* 15:26, 28.

4 The continuing debate in 2009 over whether evolution or intelligent design should be taught in schools creates conflict where none need exist. The world we know is the product of BOTH evolution and intelligent design.

5 Genesis 2:9.

6 Genesis 3:7.

7 Genesis 3:8.

Chapter 6

1 Richard Langdon, e-mail message to author, May 27, 2010.

Chapter 7

1 Guenter Wagner, "The Land of the Shadow of Death: Guenter Wagner's Near-death Experience," author's summary of near-death experience, Kevin Williams website, www.near-death.com.

2 Ibid.

3 Wright, *Evolution of God,* 18, 22.

4 Wright, *Evolution of God,* 29, 31.

5 My memories of how and why the natural wonders of the world and

structures like them were build did not survive my return to the body.

Chapter 8

[1]   John Dominic Crossan and Jonathan L. Reed, *Excavating Jesus: Beneath the Stones, Behind the Texts* (New York: HarperCollins, 2001), 11-12. Dr. Crossan is a Professor Emeritus of Religious Studies at DePaul University, Chicago, and has written 25 books on the historical Jesus and Paul. He was an ordained Catholic priest from 1957-1969. Dr. Reed is a Professor of Religion at the University of La Verne, California. He is a leading authority on early Christianity and the Sayings Gospel Q.

[2]   Wright, *Evolution of God*, 106-108.

[3]   Friedman, *Who Wrote the Bible?* 25, 61, 122, 188.

[4]   Wright, *Evolution of God*, 109.

[5]   Azmina Suleman, *A Passage to Eternity* (Alberta, Canada: Amethyst Publishing, 2004), 60-61.

Chapter 10

[1]   Quotation taken from the case of George Rodonaia as it appears in P.M.H. Atwater, *Beyond the Light: What Isn't Being Said About Near Death Experience*, rev. ed. (Kill Devil Hills, NC: Transpersonal Publishing, 2009), 74.

[2]   Jody A. Long, J.D., "Another Look at Beings Encountered During the Near-Death Experience," Near-Death Experience Research Foundation, www.nderf.org/beingsstudy.htm.

[3]   Ehrman, *Misquoting Jesus*, 179.

[4]   Mack, *Who Wrote New Testament*, 39.

[5]   Wright, *Evolution of God*, 295-296.

[6]   Ibid., 304.

[7]   Jonathan Young, speaking on the program "Ancient Astronauts," the History Channel, May 2010.

8   Crossan, *Excavating Jesus,* 49.

9   Wray and Mobley, *Birth of Satan*, 87.

10   Mack, *Who Wrote New Testament*, 45.

11   Luke 4:16-30.

12   Crossan, *Excavating Jesus*, 30. Excavations conducted by Franciscan priests show no evidence of public buildings of any kind in Nazareth.

13   Ibid., 31.

14   Ibid., 47.

15   Ibid., 36-37.

16   Ibid., 179.

17   Mack, *Who Wrote New Testament*, 6.

18   The Gospel of John is the only one that claims to be based on eyewitness testimony, according to James H. Charlesworth in *An Essential Guide: The Historical Jesus* (Nashville: Abingdon Press, 2008), 38. Dr. Charlesworth is the George L. Collord Professor of New Testament Language and Literature and Director of the prestigious Princeton Theological Seminary Dead Sea Scrolls Project. He is an internationally recognized expert in the Apocrypha and Pseudepigrapha of the Old and New Testaments, the Dead Sea scrolls, Josephus, Jesus research, and the Gospel of John.

19   Researchers often use the more politically correct CE, meaning "common era," for AD, which means "after our Lord" in Latin. BCE, "before the common era," is used instead of BC, meaning "before Christ."

20   Charlesworth, *Essential Guide,* 18-19.

21   According to Burton L. Mack, Professor of early Christianity at the Claremont School of Christianity, the only textual material dating back to the AD 20s, while Jesus was alive, is the Sayings Gospel Q. He believes the earliest versions of the Q Gospel may represent the actual teachings of Jesus, or at least as close to the historical Jesus' message as we will ever be. Unfortunately, Dr. Mack states that the Q material forms the basis for very little of the New Testament. Mack, *Who Wrote New Testament*, 47.

²²   Charlesworth, *Essential Guide,* 41-42.

²³   Mack, *Who Wrote New Testament,* 15, Chapter 9; Robert M. Price, *The Pre-Nicene New Testament: Fifty-four Formative Texts* (Salt Lake City: Signature Books, 2006), xix, 66-67. Dr. Price is a Professor of Scriptural Studies at the Johnnie Colemon Theological Seminary, traveling lecturer for the Center for Inquiry Institute in Amherst, NY, and a Fellow of the Committee for the Scientific Examination of Religion.

²⁴   Ehrman, *Misquoting Jesus,* 22-23; Mack, *Who Wrote New Testament,* 6. The consensus seems to be that all but seven of the letters attributed to Paul were in fact written after his death by his followers.

Chapter 11

¹   Ehrman, *Misquoting Jesus,* 152-170.

²   Carmel Bell, *When All Else Fails: A Journey Into the Heart With Medical Intuition and Metatronic Energy* (Sydney, Australia: Book Pal, 2010), 282-283.

Chapter 12

¹   Mack, *Who Wrote New Testament,* 7.

²   Ibid., 49.

³   Ibid., 71.

⁴   Ibid., 45.

⁵   Price, *Pre-Nicene New Testament,* xiii. Professor Price teaches scriptural studies at Johnnie Colemon Theological Seminary, is the founding editor of the *Journal of Higher Criticism,* and a Fellow of the Committee for the Scientific Examination of Religion. He has published several books and numerous articles in academic journals.

⁶   Ibid.

Chapter 13

1   Ehrman, *Misquoting Jesus*, 149.

2   Ibid., 181-186.

3   Harris, *Understanding the Bible*; Mack, *Who Wrote New Testament?*

4   Charlesworth, *Essential Guide*, xiii-xiv.

5   Ibid., xix, 15.

6   Ehrman, *Misquoting Jesus*, 53. One example Professor Ehrman gives is the story of a woman caught in adultery brought to Jesus to see whether he will adhere to the Jewish law that decrees death by stoning. He states this story was added to the Gospel of John by later scribes (63-65). Another later addition is the passage in the Gospel of Mark about casting out demons, speaking in tongues, handling snakes, drinking poison without dying, and healing by the laying on of hands (65-68).

7   Ibid., 48.

8   Ibid., 90-91.

9   Price, *Pre-Nicene New Testament*, xix.

10   Mack, *Who Wrote New Testament*, 7-8.

Chapter 14

1   James Redfield, *The Celestine Prophecy: An Adventure* (New York: Warner Books, 1993), 22-23.

Chapter 15

1   Dannion Brinkley with Paul Perry, *Saved by the Light: The True Story of A Man Who Died Twice and the Profound Revelations He Received* (New York: Harper Paperbacks, 1994).

2   Ibid., 37.

[3]   Ned Dougherty, *Fast Lane to Heaven: A Life-after-Death Journey* (Charlottesville, VA: Hampton Roads, 2001), 252-253.

[4]   Ibid., 78.

[5]   Kenneth Ring, *Heading Toward Omega: In Search of the Meaning of the Near-Death Experience*, (New York: William Morrow, 1984), 194.

[6]   Ibid. 197.

[7]   Wright, *Evolution of God*, 186. James M. Robinson, General Editor, *The Nag Hammadi Library: The Definitive Translation of the Gnostic Scriptures Complete in One Volume* (New York: HarperCollins, 1978) is an excellent collection of the Coptic Gospels complete with explanatory introductions giving historical background.

Chapter 16

[1]   Phillip L. Berman, *The Journey Home: What Near-Death Experiences and Mysticism Teach Us About the Gift of Life* (New York: Pocket Books, 1996), 132.

Chapter 17

[1]   Interestingly, I saw on the News in January 2009 that the Catholic Church had finally reversed its position. After centuries of scientific proof of Galileo's theories, the Church restored Mr. Galilee to full membership posthumously.

BIBLIOGRAPHY

Atwater, P.M.H., *Beyond the Light: What Isn't Being Said About Near Death Experience*. Kill Devil Hills, NC: Transpersonal Publishing, 2009.

Atwater, P.M.H., *Future Memory*. Charlottesville, VA: Hampton Roads, 1999.

Bell, Carmel, *When All Else Fails: A Journey Into the Heart With Medical Intuition and Metatronic Energy*. Sydney, Australia: BookPal, 2010.

Berman, Phillip L., *The Journey Home: What Near-Death Experiences and Mysticism Teach Us About the Gift of Life*. New York: Pocket Books, 1996.

Brinkley, Dannion with Kathryn Brinkley, *Secrets of the Light: Lessons from Heaven*. New York: HarperCollins, 2008.

Brinkley, Dannion with Paul Perry, *Saved by the Light: The True Story of A Man Who Died Twice and the Profound Revelations He Received*. New York: HarperCollins, 1994.

Charlesworth, James H., *An Essential Guide: The Historical Jesus*. Nashville: Abingdon Press, 2008.

Crossan, John Dominic and Jonathan L. Reed, *Excavating Jesus: Beneath the Stones, Behind the Texts*. New York: HarperCollins, 2001.

Dougherty, Ned, *Fast Lane to Heaven: A Life-after-Death Journey*. Charlottesville, VA: Hampton Roads, 2001.

Eadie, Betty J., *Embraced by the Light*. Carson City, NV: Gold Leaf Press, 1992.

Ehrman, Bart D., *Misquoting Jesus: The Story Behind Who Changed the Bible and Why*. New York: HarperCollins, 2005.

Friedman, Richard Elliott, *Who Wrote the Bible?* New York: Harper-Collins, 1987.

General Editor, *The Nag Hammadi Library: The Definitive Translation of the Gnostic Scriptures Complete in One Volume*. New York: Harper-Collins, 1978.

Harris, Stephen L., *Understanding the Bible: A Reader's Intriduction*. New York: Mayfield Publishing, 1985.

Mack, Burton L., *Who Wrote the New Testament? The Making of the Christian Myth*. New York: HarperCollins, 1995.

Price, Robert M., *The Pre-Nicene New Testament: Fifty-four Formative Texts*. (Salt Lake City: Signature Books, 2006.

Redfield, James, *The Celestine Prophecy: An Adventure*. New York: Warner Books, 1993.

Ring, Kenneth, *Heading Toward Omega: In Search of the Meaning of the Near-Death Experience*. New York: William Morrow, 1984.

Ring, Kenneth, *Lessons From the Light: What We Can Learn From the Near-Death Experience*. Needham, MA: Moment Point Press, 1998.

Ritchie, George G. with Elizabeth Sherrill, *Return from Tomorrow*. Grand Rapids, MI: Fleming H. Revell, 1978.

Russell, Jeffrey Burton, *The Devil: Perceptions of Evil from Antiquity to Primitive Christianity*. Ithaca, NY: Cornell University Press, 1977.

Suleman, Azmina, *A Passage to Eternity*. Alberta, Canada: Amethyst Publishing, 2004.

Wray, T. J. and Gregory Mobley, *The Birth of Satan: Tracing the Devil's Biblical Roots*. New York: Palgrave Macmillan, 2005.

Wright, Robert, *The Evolution of God.* New York: Little, Brown, 2009.

Index

ABOUT THE AUTHOR

Nanci L. Danison holds a B.S. degree Magna Cum Laude with double majors in biology and chemistry, a B.A. Magna Cum Laude in Psychology, and a Doctorate in Jurisprudence. Until 1994, she was living the life of a successful trial lawyer in a large midwestern law firm. She often lectured on a national level and wrote on health law topics for the health care industry. Nanci at one time appeared on the Noon News for local TV stations in public service spots for the Bar Association, one of the activities that earned her a Jaycees' "Ten Outstanding Citizens Award" for community service. Then she had a near-death experience (NDE).

After returning from beyond, Nanci left the security of her big firm and started a successful solo practice in health law. Her activities post-NDE include being named in the *1998 Who's Who in American Law*, earning a pilot's license in 2000, and being listed in the *2006 Bar Registry of Preeminent Lawyers*. Nanci still practices law and writes books on what she remembers from her life in the Light.